A Highly Ramified Tree

Other books by Robert Canzoneri:

"I Do So Politely": A Voice from the South
Watch Us Pass
Men with Little Hammers
Barbed Wire and Other Stories

A Highly Ramified Tree

Robert Canzoneri

The Viking Press • New York

First published in 1976 by The Viking Press
625 Madison Avenue, New York, N.Y. 10022

Published simultaneously in Canada by
The Macmillan Company of Canada Limited

LIBRARY OF CONGRESS CATALOGING IN PUBLICATION DATA

Canzoneri, Robert.
  A highly ramified tree.
    1. Canzoneri, Robert—Biography.   2. Authors, American—20th century—
Biography. I. Title.
  PS3553.A58Z52   818'.5'409 [B]   76-28363
  ISBN 0-670-37205-6

Printed in the United States of America.

Acknowledgment is made to Holt, Rinehart and Winston for lines from "Directive" from
The Poetry of Robert Frost edited by Edward Connery Latham. Copyright 1947, © 1969 by
Holt, Rinehart and Winston. Copyright © 1975 by Lesley Frost Ballantine. Reprinted by
permission of Holt, Rinehart and Winston, Publishers.

Chapters X and XIV have appeared in somewhat different form in *McCall's* and the *Iowa
Review* respectively.

I gratefully acknowledge aid toward the production of this book from the Department
of English, the College of Humanities, and the Office of Research of The Ohio State
University, in the form of released time, grants-in-aid, and funds for travel. I also
gratefully acknowledge the aid of Josephine Stabile in getting Sicilian from my memory
onto the page.

Contents

A Highly Ramified Tree

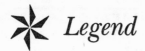 *Legend*

The distribution of the systemic arteries is like a highly ramified tree.
—Gray's *Anatomy*

A few years ago my father and I visited Palazzo Adriano, the Sicilian town in which he was born. Those days with him in the Old Country he had left two-thirds of a century before, among blood kin we hadn't known existed, stirred my awareness of the roots and branches through which we draw our sustenance. Not long afterward, a radical change in my life forced me to see roots and branches not only as means of nourishment, but as what each of us diverges into. Hence this book.

The form of my account has been influenced by a habit of mind acquired from my father, both through the blood, I suspect, and through the seat of my pants applied to a pew. If he had been teaching geography instead of preaching the gospel, he might have started with a trickle of water in Minnesota, brought three rivers together in Pennsylvania, and drained this side of the Rockies through the Great Plains just to point out Vicksburg as you swept past it down the Mississippi.

Whatever flow my life has derives in part from tributaries I have felt compelled to explore here. Since their course and the territory through which they pass is so intimately myself, I have found it useful to look back upon portions of my life as if from the outside. In several chapters the person I used to be is referred to as "he"; in one chapter a child I might have been lives in a Sicily I have had to imagine; in another a man with my name appears in an Italy which is really a state of mind.

I no more understand why these chunks of the same protoplasm grew so variously than I understand why some cells grow into brains and others into toes. Perhaps the world of our perception has some real congruence with anatomical charts; the terms, at least, are useful: in feeling my way along veins and arteries, I have hoped to discover the pattern made by the bloodstream and by the lines of blood—that is, to apprehend somewhat more clearly the shape of myself as one of millions whose lives have taken directions we did not expect.

1 *The Old Men*

In black Sicilian suits and caps they sit in the sun like a flock of blackbirds far across the piazza. One is drawn stiffly from his chair as I approach. "Roberto?"

I hurry to him. "Nino!"

He meets me, stocky as a barrel, short arms reaching up, rough whiskers against my face. The deep growl of his voice is unsteady. "Mio cugino. Sei tornato come hai promesso."

It is 1971; I have returned as I promised. We walk together through the narrow cobblestone streets, his arm around me as far as it will reach, mine down across his thick unbending back. The worn black suit is warm from the April sun. The black cap does not come up to my shoulder. I cut my steps to his and rock awkwardly from side to side. He is my cousin, old enough to be my father; the look of him, the smell and feel of him I know from my father, my dead and dying uncles, myself.

My Uncle Cyrus, in California, knows that I am in Palazzo Adriano and grinds his teeth. Monte Rose loomed over his childhood, not mine. Was it for this he told me about the Old Country? Who but he introduced me to figs as nearly like the sweet delicious fichi of Sicilia as he could find?

He sits and talks back to the television, retorts to its banality with bitter humor. What else is there to do? His wife and daughter don't want him to drive, his hands shake so on the steering wheel. They say that he is too old to have come to Sicily with me anyway; he shouts at them that he is fine. He will at least drive to Mississippi to see the older brother he loves more than anyone, my father. But he does not go.

All his life, things have worked against him. Once he had an "expensible" place in a San Fernando lemon grove, with a swimming pool, a fine garden, his older son and daughter-in-law and two grandchildren in one end of the house, he and Aunt Lena in the other. It didn't work. It was not in the United States as it was in Sicily, living always as a family, generations turning in the same spot like the wheel of his father's mill. He lost hold. He could not afford to stay when his son moved out—moved out not only from the house but from his wife and children; got divorced; married a young girl. He can accept her now; he likes her now, but there is a burning in his heart.

From the fine expensible house he went to a little house with space in the back yard for tomatoes, parsley, escarole, but his pension and social security checks were too small even for that. He and Aunt Lena live in a trailer now. Her hands are twisted with arthritis; it is painful to watch her roll the dough around bamboo sections to make cannoli, to see the pen cramped in her fingers as she tries, by writing the letters he is too impatient to write, to hold the family together.

His garden here is three rows, ten feet long—the space that the sun gets to between his and the next trailer. His sons do not take him to Sicily as I have taken my father. They do not even want to cut his hair, as I did once for him. Nobody has ever loved him as everybody loves my father. He says such things with a growl, pauses, cuts his eyes toward you, breaks into laughter. He will have a stroke, recover, have another stroke, linger, die by Thanksgiving.

Nino, his nephew in Palazzo, looks most like him. As Nino crosses the cobblestone piazza toward me in 1971, he might almost be Uncle Cyrus in 1960 coming to greet me across a California parking lot, except that Uncle Cyrus is in brown slacks and sweater, says, "Bob," instead of Roberto. Hugs me, clean-shaven. Takes me in as though he has known me all my life, as if he has seen me more than the one time a quarter-century before, when I was ten years old. Tries to pay for everything, even the film for my camera. When I protest he says indignantly, "I'ma you uncle," and shoves my money aside.

I tell Uncle Cyrus I have a friend in Long Beach I want to telephone. He does not bother to look at me. "You got a friend, you go see him." I go see him.

"You got relatives in San Jose," Uncle Cyrus says. "Go see 'em." I go. Uncle Leo, my cousins and I call him, and Aunt Ninfa. Zio Leo and zia Ninfa. They are not my aunt and uncle; she is my father's first cousin; he is kin only by marriage, but he too is from Palazzo Adriano and lived for a time in "Mississippio-and-State-of-Louisian'," where back about 1905 he and my father came down with a fever and his mother nursed them back to health in the same room. He is even smaller than my father, a year or so older, tough, illiterate. There is a scar down one cheek where a tornado threw him a hundred yards into a pile of lumber, in Illinois, in the twenties.

He talks without ceasing. At first I have difficulty making him out. "July gots, Bob?" it sounds as though he is saying. You like cots? Apricots. He thrusts a box of them upon me. "Jugo marilla tax, Bob?" he asks, swinging his thumb upward as he rises from his chair. Did I go by way of Amarillo, Texas, on my way out. No, I tell him. He did, years ago. "Jugo Sam' Fe, New Max." He makes an arc with his hand around Santa Fe. "The road she'sa no there no more, she'sa disappear."

Uncle Leo and Aunt Ninfa have just celebrated their golden wedding anniversary when I first meet them. They live in a house he built himself, not large but attractive and comfortable. The cellar is full of food—canned, bottled, fresh— enough to live on forever. He is a gardener for the rich in Los Altos Hills; they use little of what he helps grow, give him all he wants—apricots, avocados, olives. His small back yard is full of tomatoes, peppers, basil, a bearing walnut tree, and sweet lemons, sour lemons, lemons as big as your head, all on the same tree. He shows me how he "drafted" them onto the parent plant.

Uncle Cyrus—zio Ciro—drives up from Los Angeles. We sit on the back porch, Uncle Leo talking. I listen, decipher, nod. Uncle Cyrus fidgets. Now and then there is a whiff of lemon blossoms. The sun is warm on the patch of clover at our feet. Finally Uncle Cyrus can take no more. His hands gesticulate wildly, his voice is loud, angry: "Talka, talka, talka! You don't do nothing but talk alla time." The hands say it violently before he gets the next words out. "You don't know nothing. Why you talk to him for? He's gotta brainsa. He's go to schoola. You? You can'ta read you own name. Buta you *talka*." He makes a wide sweep with his arms. "Looka you! You live in a pigsty. You wife-a married to you fifty year, she'sa miserable. You don't got nothing to show for you whole life. But you *talka, talka, talka* all time don't say nothing. I can't standa no more."

He subsides. Uncle Leo sits quietly, looking at me with a faint wry smile. "You know what'sa matta you Uncle Ciro?" he says. "He'sa never grow up."

The man I knew of as Granddaddy Joe was a miller named Giuseppe Canzoneri, known in Palazzo Adriano as Peppe Gadduzzu, Little Rooster Joe. I have seen the flume from which water once fell upon his mill wheel, the charnel house among the tombs and dark cypresses where he mingles with the other dead, the garden in which he posed, stripped to the waist, as though boxing a peach tree. That photograph was the way I knew him, growing up. I could not see him in the more formal portrait taken when he was thinner, mustached, younger than I thought of my father as being. Perhaps the peach tree verified his reality. He was heavy, like my Uncle George, left arm out straight, right arm cocked. He stood erect, mocking his stance—or was it that the grandfather of a world champion would not deign to crouch? The hard little peaches hung waiting; if he struck, one would go sailing out of the picture into the Sicilian town I knew only through stories. If I had been there, a child, looking on, as soon as the shutter snapped he would have laughed, picked me up, hugged me to his whiskery face.

Only four of his more than thirty grandchildren grew up in Palazzo where he could be with them; the oldest, Sebastiano, I know only as a photograph in his house at via San Nicola N. 13, and as a tomb near our grandfather's charnel house.

Sebastiano was well into his seventies when he died shortly before my father and I visited Palazzo in 1969. Two years after his death, on my return in 1971, his daughter Felicina leads the way down a tiny dark stairway from the kitchen. "Guarditi 'a testa!" I duck my head, feel my way to the bottom. A spacious room smelling pleasantly of hay. Wine vats. On the wall a wide-brimmed hat. He wore it to the fields, Felicina says, touching it as though she were touching him. His saddle hangs nearby. He was a big man, she says. He laughed, told stories, loved people. When he was alive this room was alive with his animals, the house alive with people, with his presence. Everyone was happy. As she talks, I can feel him there, the absence of him there.

Felicina is still in black; the time of mourning for her father, my cousin Sebastiano, is not yet over, may never be over. She spreads her hands: "Now, all is silence; my mother. . . waits."

Uncle Leo has been pondering my sister's years in Nigeria

as a missionary. "Thisa religion," he says finally, "it'sa shit. You die, you go downa hole." He hangs on to life. At eighty-three he has a serious operation; next day the nurses find him up, walking the halls, keeping the muscles active. Three days later we are gathered around his bed, at home. He has moved from his little house in San Jose (he calls it Sang 'Ose) into a large new house in Los Gatos. He has already planted a garden, laid concrete walks, put in a watering system beneath the lawn. His niece, whom he raised as if she were his daughter, sits beside the bed. "I was afraid he would die," she says, "and I could just see him up in heaven shouting down, 'You forgot to water the lawn!'"

Uncle Leo turns his head on the pillow away from the others and winks at me. "Juno why I'ma no wanta go heaven, Bob? Alla my friendsa down here."

He has never been one to give in. When his friend at the driver's license bureau, who tested him for years, is retired, Uncle Leo has to learn, at eighty, to read the road signs. As soon as I come to see him, he calls me into the breakfast nook with an imperious wave of his hand, seats me opposite him, lays out a copy of the California road signs in front of each of us, puts on wire-rimmed reading glasses, pauses dramatically. "Point to a sign, Bob. Don't starta beginning. Point *any* signa."

I look at the bank of signs, maybe four or five deep, eight or ten across. I do not want him to fail, but I do not want to insult him with an easy one. I point. He peers at my finger, moves his own finger carefully to the same spot on his own copy. The lips form with great deliberation, enunciate slowly: "E . . . mer . . . gen . . . cy."

"Right!"

He waves his hand over the copies generously. "Do other sign, Bob. Any one you wanta."

We go through nearly all of them; he sounds out each, syllable by syllable. Then he stops, laying his hand on mine. "What meansa Emergency, Bob?"

"Well, it means there's danger. . . ."

His head is shaking already. "It'sa mean other cars come in froma side."

"That's Merging Traffic."

He's still shaking his head. "You wronga, Bob."

A few years later they do not tell him at the driver's license bureau that he is too old; they read the questions from one sheet and have him mark X's in squares on another; they look at the answers, say, Sorry, you'll have to come back and try again. He tries again and again. Sorry. When the man turns his back the third time, Uncle Leo rescues his answer sheet from the wastebasket. He spreads the wrinkled paper out before me—X's in boxes; nothing marked wrong or right; the questions are on a sheet he doesn't have. "I'ma give right answer, Bob." He is shaking with fury. "He'sa no tell me I'ma no pass. He'sa say, 'Sorry, come backa sometime.' " He lapses into Sicilian.

Aunt Ninfa comes out onto the porch where we sit looking out over his Los Gatos garden. "Leo!" she says. "Bob isa no unnerstand when you don't speaka English."

Uncle Leo pauses, nods knowingly at me. "He'sa unnerstand."

He seldom tells tales of his boyhood, as my father has begun to. He is interested in the future. "I'm wanna see what gonna happen next," he tells me after the first space shots. "They go to the moon, I wanna see."

Aunt Ninfa shakes her head. "They never go to the moona. God don't want them to go to the moona."

Uncle Leo ignores her. "They talk about the good olda days. It'sa shit. Three cents a loafa bread." Hands raised high. "Who's gotta three cents? You live in a shacka no windows. Don't need no windows. Gotta cracks see through outside justa same. No, Bob. Worlda better now. Lotta thing I'ma interest in." He looks out over my shoulder, caught on something I don't yet know. "Juno, Bob. I tella you something.

When I'ma gotta chick. . . ." (Some years ago he had a bar in Palo Alto, but the "bad men" began to use it as a hangout, and since there was no way to go against them he sold it and took up gardening. Before that he was a chicken farmer.) "When I'ma gotta chick, I'ma go down Sang 'Ose to getta shell for chicka. A Spaniard man gotta boat, he'sa go outa bay witha net, getta shell, grinda three gradesa, one, two, three. I'ma go down one day, the boat she'sa on dry land. I'ma say, 'What'sa matta boat?' The Spaniard he'sa say, 'What you mean, what'sa matta boat?' I'ma say, 'What'sa matta boat, she'sa on dry land?' He'sa say, 'Nothing matta boat. The water she'sa go down.' " He pauses and looks at me significantly, holds up a finger. "Once ever' twenty-four hour. She'sa go down, sometime thirty feet!" He picks up a half-full cup of coffee, holds it out toward me. "Looka, Bob." He tilts the cup. "See, she'sa go down here, and. . . ." He points across the cup to where the coffee has risen toward the rim, looks at me in wonder. "She'sa go up somewhere else ina world. Nobody isa know where."

September 11, 1969. My father is talking, I have driven southward from Palermo through Misilmeri, Marineo, Corleone. Now off to our left a town appears, grown like a gray lichen high on a mountain. "There's Prizzi!" I tell him.

"What's that?" He pulls himself out of the long narrative of some revival meeting, looks toward where I am pointing.

"Prizzi," I say. "You remember Prizzi."

"Yeah? Well I declare." He leans back in the seat and picks up the story.

I am excited by the mountainous island, like California, only more intimate, with old towns blended in. Palazzo Adriano is almost upon us, the somewhere else in the world I've heard most about and wanted most to see. My father left it as Giuseppe—Peppino, Peppineddu—when he was seventeen, in 1903; he became a Southern Baptist preacher and singer, married a Mississippi girl, devoted his life to the Lord. He was so open, happy, expressive, his accent so delightful that people found it impossible not to love him, just as they found it nearly impossible to pronounce his last name. Brother Joe, everybody came to call him.

When I told him we were going, he said, "I like to walk from Palazzo to Bivona. Be like old time." For a while his father had run a mill in Bivona, and every week my father would carry a pack of clean clothes and fresh bread to him, walking the fifteen-mile trail of crushed rock around Monte Rose.

Now, approaching Palazzo, he cannot seem to draw himself out of the long-ago revival meeting. It is as if his mind is cushioning itself against the shock of his return. We round a bend, and there it is, gray buildings with pale red tiles, atop a forepaw of Monte Rose.

"We're here," I tell him.

"What?"

"Palazzo."

The road is shut off straight ahead by buildings; we have to turn up the mountain or down. "Which way to the piazza?" I ask him.

He hesitates. "To the left. No. Down to the right."

The street opens into a wide expanse of cobblestones. The fountain he has talked about all these years is near the center. It is noon; men in dark clothes stroll together, stop, watch the strange automobile pull up, the strangers get out. "Yes," he says, about the fountain. I let him wander where he will, getting his bearings. "That's the Latin church," he says. We walk through the narrow passageway between it and the campanile. "We used to urinate here when we were boys." He looks up. I can see the town settling itself into his head. He points, already walking. "Our house was down that street."

The buildings on the left give way to a balustrade; the street is like a balcony overlooking a westward valley. "I used to watch the sunsets right here." Below us is a small chapel, vineyards, then on a hill a church and a cemetery black with cypresses. Beyond, the valley opens out for miles between mountainsides with olive groves and here and there a stone farmhouse.

Onto the balustrade beside us a hand places a mattock and a bunch of greens, and then a man pulls himself over. My father begins talking to him in Sicilian. Yes, the man responds. He remembers Peppe Gadduzzu. There are relatives here. He will wash the dirt of the garden from his hands and take us to them.

They gather rapidly in the parlor of Antonietta, widow of Sebastiano who has only recently died. He was the son of my father's oldest sister, who married when my father was perhaps four years old. She did not go to the United States. Her children, grandchildren, great-grandchildren welcome zio Peppino with a kiss upon each cheek. They bring out pictures of him—the latest with my mother when they married in 1918. They had despaired of ever seeing him. And what of the others? Zio Giorgio, they know, is dead. Zia Ninfa too? And zia Vincenzina? I make them understand that she has had a stroke, cannot speak. Ah, sad. The same with Tetina, here. But what of zio Ciro? Fine. And zio Peppino, actually here, and looking so young! It is impossible that he is eighty-three. They feel his face. "Pelle come un bambino!" He responds, delighted, with hesitant words in Sicilian, words that come too slowly; the talk sweeps around him, beyond, while he struggles.

He tries to tell them about himself, protests, laughing, "I think it in Italian, but it comes out English. You see, all my schooling was in English. I graduate from Miss'ippi College in Clinton, Miss'ippi. It's a very good college, we learn everything there." He tries to explain the exact geography of the house and two acres the Lord has been so good as to provide, but it is in a language they do not understand about a place they know only in general, the Stati Uniti, which contains Nuova Yorka, California, Chicago, Brookaleeno, and O-hee-ho, where Neil Armstrong is from. They watched him walk on the moon. Into my father's English monologue I intersperse Italian words like subtitles for a movie.

At midnight we stroll with the men in the piazza; they help us register at the little albergo and leave us for the night. My father undresses in the bare tiled room, a small man shrunk even smaller with age. His arms are thin and leathery; biceps like old lemons swell the loose skin. He wears a heavily-stayed corset for a back problem, explains the history and function of it to me at length. He is glad to be here, keeps telling me how he appreciates my having brought him, but his mind seems unable to engage the fact, his attention is distracted. His hands begin a methodical search through his suitcase for pajamas, forget what they are doing, stop. He tells me the familiar story of his coming home from a revival meeting when we were little, having decided not to bring the usual gifts. When we asked what he brought us, he answered, "Just myself," and we filed away—he acts it out, as he does everything; his shoulders sag with disappointment. "But you come back—just a little bitty thing—and take my thumbs." Thumbs go out, hands grasp around little hands no longer there. "Remember how you used to do that? And walk up me and hug my neck. And I say, 'What you want, Bob?' And you say. . . ." He shakes his head. "I never forget it long as I live. You say, 'I just want you.'" His face stiffens; he turns away, clears his throat. After a moment his hands fumble in his suitcase again. I can smell again the leather of that other suitcase, feel the arms tight around me, the rough face against mine.

He keeps forgetting what it is he is looking for, forgetting that he has told the story, going through it again. I am propped up in my narrow bed against the wall; I keep urging him to go to bed too. It is very late. Finally he stands there, puzzled. "This *is* Palazzo, isn't it? Where I was born?"

"Yes."

He shakes his head. "I keep thinking there are two Palazzos."

"No. There's just this one."

"One where I was born, and . . . this one."

"There's just this one. You'd better get some sleep, Dad."

He nods, takes a deep breath. "Well. Goodnight, son." He kneels on the tile floor to say his prayers.

Next morning he tells me, "That was foolish, about two Palazzos." He pours water from the pitcher on the washstand into the heavy bowl and splashes his face. "That man say last night I'm supposed to have my birth certificate."

He's talking about the albergatore, when we registered. "He just said your passport doesn't say you were born in Palazzo. It only says Italy."

"But I get in trouble without my birth certificate. He was talk about. . . ."

"He just hadn't realized this was your hometown until you told him, and he was explaining that he hadn't said anything about it because the passport just said Italy."

He dries his face, stands there uncertainly. "He say something about birth certificate."

"No, just birthplace. All you need is your passport."

Slowly, methodically he gets dressed. "Social security supposed to have my birth certificate. They ask me, but I never get it for them."

He has, of course, been getting social security for years. But I can see now that he is struggling to deal with the two Palazzos in his head, the one sixty-six years gone, the other so present that he can touch its stones. He has to bring them together like the two images in the viewfinder of my camera, so that the world will be in focus again.

My cousins nod knowingly at the request I have formulated from the dictionary; they take us to the municipio at the lower end of the piazza. We go up wide stairways, past plain offices that might almost be in a county courthouse back home. The man in the records office listens patiently, nods. What year? I stammer it out: "Mille ottocento ottantasei." He pulls a ledger from a bookcase and spreads it open for us to see. There it is: 24 settembre 1886. Giuseppe, son of Giuseppe Canzoneri and Antonina LoBurgio. The clerk types up two copies, refuses pay, congratulates my father on his eighty-third birthday less than two weeks off.

We go out into the sun again. My father points to a balcony we are walking past. "Used to be a beautiful girl lived there, used to come out and smile at me. My father was afraid we gonna run away and get married." He laughs, looks up at the deep blue sky. "He sent me to Bivona for a while."

The sky is very clear in Palazzo, the air pure. It is pleasant to cross the street every morning and meet some of our relatives at the little bar. "Bella giornata," I learn to say. "Cielo azzurro. Aria fina."

And my father always says, "Reminds me of the old song Caruso used to sing." He spreads his arms, his face lights up, he begins, "Che bella cosa. . . ." They join in for the rest of the line—" 'na iurnata e sole"—take our arms and lead us inside for espresso. My father will not put sugar in his. He swallows it down, looks at the small thick cup. "They don't put much coffee in there, do they?"

Every night when we return to the hotel after the midnight stroll in the piazza, he stands in the middle of the room and talks. "I'm get old, the blood doesn't get to my brain sometimes." He tells familiar stories about his boyhood, revival meetings, college days. "You know, maybe I told you, one time I didn't bring you kids anything when I come back from a revival meeting. . . ." I learn that the only way to get him to bed is to doze off while he is talking.

No one listens to old Tony Tuzzolino, who sits in the other Palazzo bar, the one with the grape arbor out front surrounded by oleanders. He is drinking something from a cup. The men of the town razz him in Sicilian as he talks to me in English. "They are ignorant," he says. " I'd rather be in jail in the United States than free in Palazzo Adriano."

"Getting drunk again today, eh Tony?" They poke fingers at him. "Show him how to shoot a man."

His hand trembles. "I used to read their letters, write their letters, so many have relatives in America. Now," he points to his clouded eyes, "I can't read my own."

Some say that years ago in Texas he killed two or three Mexicans who cheated him at gambling; he says only, "I led a bad life." Listening to his soft accent I might as well be in a beer joint back home. He went to the United States when he was only two years old; he was deported in 1945. "They brought us ashore in Naples," he says. "Three of us and a guard, trying to get some food. But it was right after the war and the people were starving. Rats everywhere, big as dogs. But you know, they shared what little they had with us. It was pitiful."

"Bang, bang," his compatriots are saying. "Are you a tough man, Tony?"

He sips from the cup, looks away from them. "Pitiful."

The only relative of my father's generation remaining in Palazzo is a tiny man, Carmelo Canzoneri. My father is about five-three; Carmelo is much smaller. They meet in the piazza and my father tries to remember back. "I had a cousin named Ciro, used to play all kind of pranks with me." He is speaking English. I get down to take a picture, but Carmelo holds his hand out before the lens. "Niente fotografia," he says. He reaches into the inside pocket of his limp coat and pulls out a sheaf of what appear to be 4x5 cards, hands one to my father. It is a studio portrait of himself.

That evening at Antonietta's house, or Nino's, or Giuseppina's, my father turns to me. "Who was that little bitty man in the piazza?"

"That was your first cousin."

"Oh." He thinks a minute. "What was his name?"

"Carmelo. Carmelo Canzoneri."

"Oh, yeah." He shakes his head. "Such a pitiful little man."

The younger Carmelo Glaviano (there are two), twenty-six, fun-loving, generous, is driving through the Sicilian countryside, singing in a nasal voice somewhat off-key. My father sits beside him, suffering. Finally he says, "You need to breathe right, from the diaphragm." He launches into one of his favorite lectures, How to Sing.

From the back seat I lean toward him. "Tell him in Sicilian."

"Oh, yeah." He thinks a minute. "Hai bisogno . . . learn to breathe. . . ." He cannot wait for the words. The lesson goes on in English for ten, fifteen, twenty mountainous kilometers. Now and then Carmelo grasps what sounds like Sicilian, the ending of one word coupled to the beginning of another. "You need to warm up your vocal cords, too. You shouldn't try to do robust songs first thing."

Do ro-bust. Do-ro. "Duro," Carmelo says. "Si."

When the lecture ends, Carmelo picks up singing again.

"You really should try it in Sicilian," I tell my father. "He doesn't understand."

He adjusts his back straight in the seat of the Fiat. "Well, I think some of it is getting through. He's singing better now."

He loves being in Palazzo, but he keeps telling them, "I can't wait to get back to my li'l girl." My mother is half a dozen years younger than he. He tells them how good a cook she is, how she makes the best spaghetti in the world. Friends come from Clinton and eat dinner with them on Sunday. He tries to tell his Sicilian relatives how good the Lord has been to him, how they should trust Christ as he has. He sings "O Sole Mio" to them and then sings the words he wrote to the tune, about how Jesus died for him. In English.

On a typical evening, he is carrying on a monologue directed toward Nino, who happens to be sitting nearest, while I struggle to understand what Giovanna is saying to me and try to throw Nino an explanatory word from time to time. I gather that Giovanna is telling me about something we may get tomorrow, but I don't catch much of it through my father's monologue:

"My brother George go down Independence, Louisiana, and I go there too, from New York City. So then he run a mill over in Lumberton, Miss'ippi, and I work in a barber shop there. But the mill close down and he leave, so I take a barber shop in Purvis, Miss'ippi, not far away."

I say, "Barbiere," to Nino, who gives a vague nod, and to Giovanna, "Non capisco." She begins again, very slowly and distinctly, as my father continues:

"Fellow name Collins I room with say go to Sunday School with him. I dint know what is, but I get this hunger I want go to school. He say in Sunday School they study the Bible, and I never see a Bible before."

I tell Nino, "Scuola, uh, domenica," and signal Giovanna to go on, hoping I'll catch later what thing it is we'll go get tomorrow.

"So I try read," my father is saying, "look in dictionary near 'bout every word, and I find out God love the world, and send his Son. And I say, Lord, you mean you not want to punish us all time, not mad at us? And I see I been making a devil out of God, I dint know he love people."

Nino is stolid patience itself, but he cuts his eye at me, and I say, "Dio." He nods. Giovanna is saying that whatever we'll go to get is on the road to Bisacquino, not far from Nino's garden.

"Well, I struggle for a long time before I say, Lord, take me. I believe Jesus die to save me, and I accept him in my heart. T.T. Martin preach in meeting there, I join the church. I feel so good, I declare I never forget it. You see, Columbus discover America, lot of rocks and trees, but I discover a person, Jesus Christ, live inside of me ever since."

"Salvatore," I inform Nino. I decide that I have to find out what Giovanna is talking about or be forever lost. "Che cosa?" I ask her. "Non capisco che cosa troviamo vicino il giardino."

"Racina," Giovanna says. "Racina molto saporita."

By the time I get the question out and she answers, my father has taken his story far enough for me to feel obliged to give Nino another subtitle: "So I start school," he has said, "twenty-four years old in fifth grade, only pretty soon they say I can't stay out late and lead the singing in revival meeting, but I have to do what God say, and they kick me out. Then I go up to Miss'ippi College in Clinton, Miss'ippi, the academy there, and the Lord help me. . . ."

"Scuola," I tell Nino. "Uh, collegio."

". . . I declare, I never make it if he dint."

"Dad," I say, stuck on Giovanna's key word, "what does racina mean?"

"Had what?"

"Racina. What does it mean?"

He nods in approval. "Racina. That's right."

"What does it mean, though?"

He exaggerates the pronunciation: "Rah-CHEE-nah. You see, when it is c before i, you say CHEE: Rah-CHEE-nah."

"That's what I'm saying. But what is it in English?"

He nods, turning back to Nino's patient ear. "It's the same thing."

Giovanna smiles. "Racina è una parola siciliana. È uva in italiano." She points to my pocket. "Dizionario."

I check uva in the little dictionary and begin to see the logic. Grapes is grapes, whatever the language.

They are building a road to Bivona. It curves out above the town, climbs a distance up Monte Rose, swings around her to the west and ends, not yet over the pass, just beneath the old ruined chapel of San Calogero. Some of the younger folk go with us there one day, help my father up the steep slope. He looks at the few chunks of rock underfoot with what seems to me his usual interest in everything, climbs on to the chapel, looks at the crumbling stone, the view far over Palazzo to Prizzi high in the distance. I motion the girls to pose for a picture with the valley in the background. The wind whips their skirts and the scarf tying up Tina's hair. When I turn back, Pippo is signaling me not to speak. He points to my father a little below us, stooped slightly over an old path of crushed stone. As if he gets a clear scent, suddenly he is off down the road he used to travel from Bivona to Palazzo. "It crosses the new road a few meters back toward town," Pippo says. "Wait in the car there."

They come into view over a rise, my father striding, Pippo walking within reach. He opens the door; my father gets in; we drive back down the mountain.

24 settembre 1969. In two days Pippo will be twenty-one. Tomorrow Nino will be seventy-one. On this his last day in Palazzo, my father is eighty-three. Nearly two dozen of us crowd into Nino's house, eat thick pizza, toast each other with sweet white wine, cut the large cake they have ordered from the bakery in Chiusa Sclafani. They toast my father, seated at the table between his nephew Nino and his niece Giuseppina, wish him a happy compleanno. He never drinks; he has preached against it for more than half a century. I do not know whether it is absent-mindedness, reversion to older times, or a sense of family that brings the glass to his lips. He stands and begins to speak, slowly and clearly, in Sicilian. He tells them that they can never know how much it means to him to have come home to them, to get to know them and love them. His face twists. He bites his lip, sits down. Nino's face distorts. Little Carmeluccia has wadded up a paper napkin and throws it at little Tina. Suddenly everybody is laughing and paper wads fill the air.

The good-byes have been said, but the next morning when we drive through the piazza to leave, Nino is there. He has been waiting two hours. He comes across to us, his hand up, to be sure we do not get away. He gets in and rides to the edge of town. I look back and he is still standing where we left him, watching us drive out of sight. I have told him I will return in '71.

"Promesso?"

"Promesso." I cannot promise that my father will be back.

In Rome, he begins telling a man his life story. "I'm sorry," the man says to me. "I don't speak Italian." He is an Iranian who attended Utah State University.

"In English," I tell my father. "He speaks English." But the Sicilian so long dammed up has broken loose. The stranger is rescued by a bus.

On the plane to New York I am sitting between my father and a soprano with the New York City Opera. She has been to Germany where they want her to make some appearances, and has stopped off in Rome because she loves it. She will not return to Germany despite generous offers, beautiful theaters, accomplished performers, an artistic atmosphere she has always dreamed of. She will not leave her family for that long a time. Both her father and her father-in-law came from Sicily. "These old Sicilian men," she says. "There's something about them." One of them has taken up violin making and Russian in his eighties.

I tell my father she is an opera singer and he is immediately interested. I get up and work my way back to the rest room. When I come back, my father is leaning across my seat, talking. "You see," he is saying, hand on diaphragm. "You gotta breathe from here."

2 Road Home

My father begins to recall many things about Palazzo Adriano when he realizes, during the summer of 1969, that he will return—the teacher who beat him, outings with the family to some huge rock with steps carved into it—but his memories center upon the house he grew up in. He tells about his father's punishing him there: "He could be a hard man, but he love us. He send me out the door and say to go away if I gonna be bad. I was just a little bitty thing, and it was dark, and cold. I sat down right by the house, where the stones were built up from the road there, and miserable! I was just sick. So finally Feliciuzza happen to come by, my older sister, married already and live not far away. She take me inside and bless my father out, and he let me back. He hug me, I never forget it. He didn't mean any harm. He try to correct us."

Or he remembers the time he was in the upper room of the house and fell asleep between two mattresses. "They look all over town for me, think something awful happen to me. When I wake up, it scare them to death. But they grab me and take on over me, they're so glad I'm all right." The house is the place, he has decided; we'll go there first thing and knock on the door.

"What if it's not there?" my mother says. "That was a long time ago."

22

He looks at her a moment. "The house still there," he says. How can she picture what she has never seen? Buildings with stone walls two feet thick are not tenant shacks, built to be abandoned. Palazzo isn't an American city, constantly wrecking and rebuilding. In the Old Country houses have not become so thin and impermanent that they can be fitted with wheels and never touch down.

He remembers that after their father died, his brother George sent papers to be signed, turning the house over to their stepmother. During the last years of her life (he must have heard this years ago, through Uncle George; he has not kept in touch) a daughter of his sister Feliciuzza moved in and cared for her. He thinks maybe the niece was given the house; maybe she lives there still.

I am sure that if I write to Palazzo—to the mayor, to whom it may concern, to anybody—whatever family remains will be all set to entertain us. But I want this to be my father's trip. If I tell his younger brother, Cyrus, he will want to come along; my father will be pulled where Cyrus wants to go, will be plagued by his contrary memories. I can take Uncle Cyrus later, I think, and I will give no one in Palazzo notice. If my father wants to go to the house first, that's where we'll go.

When we arrive in Palazzo, my father leads me down through the piazza onto the road that eventually zigzags out of town, dips through the long valley, and rides the folds of the mountainside toward Bisacquino and Chiusa Sclafani. He goes to where the house is, but it has been replastered and there is new stonework where it rises above the roadway; he stands, looking all around. "It's right here, someplace," he says tentatively.

The man coming home from his garden takes us to our Sicilian relatives; they turn out to be as concerned as I that my father be given his head. That afternoon, sons of my cousins escort us back through cobblestone streets and knock on the door for us. A woman invites us in and shows us three small rooms. "Used to be just one big room downstairs," my father says. The upstairs is now separate, a house of its own. From its balcony, over the door through which we have entered, a gray-haired woman leans beside her pot of basil and watches us without speaking. We do not knock at her door, level with the street on the uphill side, but we stop.

"We kept the animals in there," my father says, pointing to the back of the house. "One time I caught a chicken and took it to my stepmother's father, 'way over in Burgio. I heard he was sick. My stepmother tried to make me not go, but I love that man like he was my own grandfather. I never forget that walk through the woods, with crosses where people had been killed, and some dogs got after me, and I arrive in Burgio at night and hear somebody moan down the street, so I find my way around through other streets—they lure you sometimes that way and knock you in the head. I find out later it was a man hurt there, die I think. And I saw in a window the biggest fight, a man and a woman throwing pots and chairs, everything they could get their hands on. I stay and watch awhile, and I laugh, it was funny to me at that time. When I finally get to my grandfather—must be after midnight—he say, 'What on earth you doing here?' and hug me." My father shakes his head. "I never forget it. He love me too, that old man. I took him a chicken. My stepmother came out and try to stop me."

He is still standing before the door she came out of seventy years before. The two Carmelo Glavianos and Pippo Alessi wait patiently. He is speaking English. He will stand in one spot until our backs ache, unless I get him in motion toward where I hope he wants to go. I take his arm. "You ready to go back, Dad?"

"Back? We going back home now?"

"No. Just up to Antonietta's house."

"Fierce dogs," he says, moving slowly up the cobblestones. "Use them to guard the sheep. I thought they gonna tear me up."

He was born in that house. His birth certificate says so: on

via Florio, 24 settembre 1886. I was born in a hospital in San
Marcos, Texas, November 21, 1925, according to my mother's
sworn testimony. By 1969 when I applied for a passport, my
birth had vanished from official records.

Two months after I was born, my father resigned as voice
teacher at San Marcos Academy and took the family "back" to
Mississippi. We moved into a house near Clinton, but the site
of my first memory is my grandparents' house in Standing
Pine, where my mother was born. A low white house with a
gallery across the front, thin white posts, a swing, rocking
chairs. Two rooms on each side of a wide hallway and, stuck
out behind on the right, a dining room and a kitchen with a
porch alongside. A wooden cupboard called a safe, with the
constant odor of pound cake through the holes punched in its
metal panels. A black wood-burning cookstove. Coffee fresh
from the grinder on the wall, biscuits in the oven, butter soon
to come from the thumping churn. Of course, these impres-
sions are from many childhood visits. That very first memory
takes in considerably less; it is of my father's knee; I am running alongside it, and I can see square-trimmed boxwoods lining the sandstone walkway to the front step.

That house is still there, too, renovated. I took my new wife
to see it recently; my uncle's widow now owns it; she and her
new husband were not at home. The old well house has been
gone for years, as have the barns, the chicken house, the pig-
pen. There is a carport at the end of the gallery. The damp
sandy clay underneath the back rooms, where we used to play
out of the hot sun, has been enclosed. If my mother's birthplace were not virtually the only house in sight, if it were
crowded in among narrow streets as my father's birthplace is,
I would not recognize it.

From the house in Palazzo you can look westward over part
of the wide valley and see the Church of the Madonna delle
Grazie on an opposing hill, and just below it a cemetery with

cypresses, where my grandfather and grandmother are buried, nameless, among other dead in a low charnel house. From my mother's birthplace you can walk a few hundred yards down a road to the little graveyard where my grandfather and grandmother lie beneath a double headstone; my grandmother cared for it a quarter of a century before someone carved the final date under her name. Nearby, a stand of tall pines all in a line used to rise from bare pastureland; I thought then that they must be what gave the community its name. Now, if they are there, they are obscured by second growth.

As many times as I have driven to Standing Pine, I have always had more trouble finding it than I did locating Palazzo the first time, in 1969. In Sicily the only difficult part was getting out of Palermo. All I knew was to bear eastward to where the map showed a highway turning inland. We were nearly out of the city before I located the street markers: marble plaques set in buildings like cornerstones. Even then I couldn't both read them and maneuver through the wild traffic. When the broad street I had settled upon divided ahead, I pulled over beside a tiny newsstand, worked up a halting question: "Dov'è la strada a Misilmeri?"

The man shrugged, shook his head. "Tedesco," he said.

I waited for some German to make itself known to me. Nothing. "Français?" I said.

"Oui," Blank. The half-dozen phrases of Italian I had pounded into my head apparently displaced all other foreign languages. "Rue," I heard myself say finally. "Rue, uh, Misilmeri."

He pointed. Soon we were on the highway, and it was easy to follow the signs and milestones. I had not expected Sicily to be so mountainous, with never a level, straight stretch of road. Now and then a tiny Fiat would careen toward us around a blind curve, horn beeping madly. I pressed on as fast as I dared, as though Palazzo might disappear on the stroke of noon.

The highway to Prizzi turns off at Corleone, climbs around the city into a long tunnel with openings through which can be seen tall campanili and a huge rock capped with what appears to be an ancient fortress. When we took the road off to the right below Prizzi, where the sign points to Palazzo Adriano, my father was telling about some revival meeting for which he had led the singing. Without slowing down, I took a one-handed picture of a flock of long-haired sheep the shepherd had driven across the road just ahead of us. My father talked on; the countryside must have been as much a blur to him at that moment as it turned out to have been for the camera. But this was not the road he remembered. The roads he knew were for feet, for the hooves of mules. He had seen men with hammers crush rock for them by hand. They were laid over the terrain like paths, not tunneled, cut, graded, blacktopped. We had driven into the town itself before he could get it into his head that we were actually in territory that he had wandered as a boy.

There's a paved road to Standing Pine now, too, which alters the territory I rode through as a boy and drove through as a man trying to find my grandmother's house. Unmarked gravel and clay roads ran over the low hills like the lines of a jigsaw puzzle, wandered among pine thickets and fields of scrawny cotton, connecting hardly definable places like Freeny, Madden, Good Hope. "Just stay on this road," people used to tell me. "Can't miss it." A few hundred yards farther along, inevitably, the road would divide into identical branches. I half believe the fantasy that grew out of countless futile inquiries: I stop at the edge of a worn ditch, lower the window, shout through the drifting dust and a barbed wire fence to a farmer turning his mule at the end of a row. "Please, sir, can you tell me the way to Standing Pine?"

He hitches at the plow, makes a low sound in his throat to the mule, steps to the fence, peers into the car at me. "Standing Pine?"

"Yes. I seem to be lost."

"Well, it's right up the road a piece. You visiting some of your folks?"

"My grandmother."

He peers even more closely. "Barnett? Miss Tessie?"

"That's right."

"You must be one of Mabel's boys."

"Yes, I am. But I can't seem to find the right road."

He stands looking at me yet another moment before his arm rises and he is pointing. "Just go on the way you're headed, and turn right, oh, about a quarter mile this side of Ole Man Lambert's cotton house." He shakes his head. "Course I mean where it used to be." He takes off his wide straw hat, wipes his forehead with his sleeve, squints up at the sun. "Can't miss it," he says.

These roads were laid on the existing surface, for the most part, like the Sicilian mule trails, and it was fun when we were children to speed up over the abrupt rises and get "that funny feeling" as the bottom fell out. When it rained, which was often, the hills were slick and treacherous; if you didn't make it to the top your first try, you learned to let your car roll backward in its tracks; try to control it and you'd spin into the ditch. Scott Hill, down past the graveyard toward my Great-uncle Oscar's house, was the hill of them all. I remember my father's slipping and sliding us up it in our Model A Ford when half the road had caved into the ditch.

The paved roads confused me even more than usual, the last trip to Standing Pine. We doubled back and doubled back until finally, from what seemed an impossible direction, we came to where the two or three stores are. It took me a while to get the world turned straight in my head. The blacktop runs through town and on beyond my grandmother's house almost to the graveyard, to where the road swings off past Otis Wright's house and over Standing Pine Creek in sight of the swimming hole Uncle Chester took me to when I was a boy. He stood with me near the bridge and watched some men seine what they called a bar pit and bring up a large bass. "Against the law," my uncle told me.

The graveyard is fenced, now. Hedged, planted, kept neat. There are several marble headstones I had never seen, including one for Uncle Chester. I couldn't locate the grave of the Civil War deserter, dug north-south instead of east-west, so that he could not rise like decent folk on the day of judgment. I had wanted to show it to my wife.

"Let's go down Scott Hill," I told her. "I'm sure it's not much, but it used to seem big." It turned out to be like dropping off the world—even steeper and higher than I remembered. We turned around at a farm far more prosperous than any in my memory, and I felt somehow vindicated that we had to coax our Volkswagen up the hill to get away.

The house I grew up in stood exactly between Jackson and Clinton, Mississippi, but the road I grew up on was really between Savannah, Georgia, and San Diego, California—U.S. 80, stretching all the way across the unimaginable continent. A step in either direction was a step toward a distant ocean—just stay on the road; you can't miss it. Not long ago I met someone who grew up on the same street, five hundred miles away, in west Texas.

The road is still two lanes of blacktop, but it is no longer the highway. Some thirty-five or forty years ago they moved the U.S. 80 signs to a new, modern, concrete strip a mile or two behind us. My older brother helped put it in, driving a dump truck. Now it is worn and narrow, and farther south still is the functional coast-to-coast Interstate 20. Our road is just Clinton Boulevard, no longer the only paved road between

Jackson and Clinton; people take the interstate, or 80, or Northside Drive, or they swing clear around by Camp Kickapoo to get from a complex of office buildings to a complex of suburban homes where there were only woods and pasture a few years ago. But Clinton Boulevard was the only way to leave the house I grew up in, and it is still the only way to return.

For several years after we moved into the house, the front yard dropped off abruptly into a still older roadbed, a wide, weed-grown stretch between us and the pavement. Eventually my father had it filled and terraced so that it became part of the huge yard he mowed until, at eighty-five, his legs would no longer keep up with the mower. The oaks that used to stand in line in front of the house, above the drop-off to the old roadbed, have been gone for years. Now, down near where the driveway meets Clinton Boulevard, there is another oak tree, so large and established it is hard to imagine that it, and the thick wisteria growing up its trunk, sprouted where the road once was; hard to visualize my father steering Model T's through heavy gravel where the tree now stands, when he drove jitneys to pay his way through college; hard to accept that the tree's weathered bark is younger than my skin.

 *Roses*

I used to see those jitney days, when my father and mother met, as through a picture painted on a gauze curtain, an oval portrait of Carrie Jacobs Bond copied from the cover of her sheet music. She is seated like Whistler's mother, but she is not stark and her dress is not black. Her tender face, her hair pulled into a bun, her long dress, all are soft and full, all in pale shades of the end of a perfect day. Long-stemmed red roses, subdued in the dusky light, stand before her in a tall vase, touching the rim of the painted oval. When the lights come up beyond the scrim, the scene is as the world once looked to veiled young ladies: lines softened, perspectives diminished to backdrops, colors perversely brightened.

Through the Gate

Posed in his college-yearbook suit with the scant coat curved back like a cutaway from its single button, his wavy black hair in a fashionable pompadour, he is caught by the bright movement of girls playing. One girl is tall and supple; she has a soft oval face, but her features are finely formed, her eyes intelligent. That is the girl I am going to marry, he tells himself. The gate closes. She is shut off by the high board wall surrounding the girls' college; the green campus and rambling white buildings are so vivid that they tint the sky above them. Laughter floats over the wall. He stands very still, distinguishing her voice from the others'. The narrow concrete walk to the house stretches now like a tightrope over a waterfall, but he forces his feet to try it. He does not go to his room, but finds Mrs. Hamilton in the kitchen. "There's a girl," he says. "I want you to find out who she is."

Whisper of Pines

Now he is in a striped shirt with a narrow collar. Three Model T's fan out between the Hamilton house and the high board fence. He is sitting in the driver's seat of one, his foot out on the running board. A tall young man leans on the next, telling a story about a gathering near his home when he was a boy, how somebody pulled a gun and shot someone, and how he took off running so fast that his foot hit the bridge over Standing Pine Creek only once in the middle.

The short man with the wavy black pompadour laughs, watching him. This is the brother of the girl he saw through the gate, the girl whose presence he can feel even now through the board wall. He and her brother drive jitneys for Mr. Hamilton, taking professors to their preaching engagements some Sundays, driving students from the men's college to Jackson and back. He has told no one but Mrs. Hamilton about the girl, and now he is listening to her brother, whom he has known all along. He is trying to picture the place called Standing Pine, the creek, the road to her home. His own home, the house of his childhood, is thousands of miles away, in Sicily. It is built of stone; the cobblestone street comes to its front door, turns uphill to its corner, goes so steeply up its side that you can step into the doorway of the second story. From the westward window he used to watch the sun set beyond the mountains, see it tint the whole long valley dusky red so that something would pull at his heart the way the thought of the girl does now. Her house in Standing Pine will be of wood. There will be no mountains. The air will be sweet with the smell of pine.

A Lesson in Music

Once a week he is allowed to walk through the gate in his pegged trousers, one-button jacket, thin bow tie. Under his arm he carries a heavy sheaf of music, and he must go directly to the rambling white building where his voice teacher will be carelessly fingering the piano keys while she gazes into the dim recesses of the hall, waiting. He walks slowly, eyes alert. He glimpses only a white pinafore scurrying between distant buildings.

Now a girl in a pale dress with a square collar is angling toward his path, a tall girl with her hair piled in a mound. Her face is sweet. She sees him but does not look directly at him, nods but does not speak. She turns onto the walk ahead of him, perfection itself, the Gibson girl sanctified by this pure and holy place. He knows who she is—no longer a student, but a graduate of this college, a young woman of impeccable character now charged with the morals of the young ladies following in her footsteps. For the moment he is following in her footsteps; he watches her smooth motion, the startling little heartbeat of her feet within the long skirt. She would grace the home of any man called to do God's work. Why does he not follow faster? Why do his eyes keep darting from side to side? He is a student and she is not, but he is half a dozen years older. She is taller than he, but so is the girl his eyes are seeking.

Girls come streaming out of a classroom, see him, and shy like a flock of birds. His eyes flick from face to face: no, no, no, no, no. One girl giggles behind her hand and turns away; another sticks out her tongue, her eyes bold upon him.

He goes into the dim hall, feels his way down the aisle to the low stage where his voice teacher awaits him. The notes she strikes are low; they reverberate in the wooden floor, the wooden walls, the wooden chairs; they are as dark in tone as the air in the unlighted hall. The voice teacher takes her hand off the keyboard, puts it to her face. She has not looked at him and does not now. "Joe," she says, "you have a beautiful voice. People love you. God surely led you to this country and to this place because he has great things in store for you."

She stands, still looking into the hall. She is straight and slender, dressed in black, imperious. She turns to him. "All right. Mi, mi, mi, up and down the scale." Through the window he can see a widening strip of green which at any moment the girl may be led to cross.

The Reception

The wall is lined with responsible eyes, the corners gleam with them. Bunting sways in long strips from the center of the ceiling; she stands underneath as though all things radiate from the spirit which hovers like an angel above her. Joe wants to go to her, but he must wait for the games which will pair them as if by chance. He does not believe in chance; God will provide, as God has led him through all these years to this place, to this time, to this one girl now chatting with another girl, eyes flicking once his way, once across the room to someone else.

It is the president of his class, the one voted most likely to succeed, the favorite of everyone. He stands watching the girl, arms crossed, one leg cocked slightly aside as though posing for a photograph. Casually he turns away, strolls behind a booth labeled Fish Pond: cane poles lean upward against a rod wrapped in blue and gold; strings drop out of sight behind a stretch of cardboard cut in waves and painted blue. Hands behind his back, he gazes slowly around the room. At every turn his eyes brush across the back of the cardboard sea. Soon he reaches up as though to straighten a line, watches what bobs beneath, marks with his eyes the pole attached. The heavy chaperon nearby has pursed her lips. He winks at her; she looks aside. Ostentatiously, he yawns, then strolls back toward the girl.

Joe looks on, bewildered. God has promised him this girl. He cannot let a boyish prank keep them apart, this first chance to be together. Even now she looks his way, and the glance sets him in motion. He stops behind the Fish Pond, looks at the row of cut-out hearts dangling there on safety pins. He knows from watching the class president where he will find her name, and there it is in fine black script on red construction paper: Mabel.

A tall chaperon with tiny gold-rimmed glasses trills for attention. All eyes turn her way, away from him. His heart is pounding so he cannot breathe. He brushes imaginary dust from his pegged trousers; as if it drifts upon the shoes he has polished with such vigor to so perfect a shine, he stoops behind the cardboard sea. His hands are not steady, but he swaps her heart to another pole, one quirked up like a finger crooked to say, Come here. His hand is alive with the touch of her name. When he rises, the muscles jump in his legs.

"The time has come," cries the thin chaperon. Elbowing his jocular way to the front, the president calls out, "First choice," and pretends to set the hook. While the president swoops about the room as though pulled by a running trout, Joe lifts the beckoning pole and brings to his hand the fluttering heart.

Soon he stands with her at a table draped in white; they sip grape punch from crystal glasses. Her dress is the color of ripe peaches, the color of her cheeks. Her eyes, and his, are blue.

The Promise

There are two beds in the small infirmary. One is empty, flat, with white sheets tightly cornered. She is in the other, mortified, spotted all over with precise red dots, face flushed with gentle fever.

One of the twin rows of girls on the way to church is incomplete. The gap in the line strikes him like a blow to the face. All through the hymns he loves, his mind is alert only to an unformed question, his rich baritone follows notes without timbre, sings words without meaning. He does not know what the preacher is saying; it is as if all the English he has learned has been knocked out of his head.

He watches the files of girls leave church, hoping he is mistaken. But, no, she is not there. He is drawn behind them along brick streets, under elm trees. He watches as the gate opens, the girls in their light spring dresses disappear, the gate closes. Down the narrow concrete walk he runs, bursts through the door, hurries to the kitchen. "Mrs. Hamilton," he says.

She stands at the sink. "I've already asked," she tells him.

In the infirmary, the girl turns her face aside on the cool pillow. Measles, at her age! If he finds out, she will die. It will be another whole week before she can see him again, pass him as she walks to church and pass him again as she returns. He will be close to the walk, his hair black and wavy, his face not pale and tinged with blood like the others', but touched with olive. If she were bold, she would reach out and touch his hand. Today, with her not there, he will have noticed some other girl in the line, one not so tall, one sweet-faced, soft, pretty. Next Sunday that is where his eyes will be. At the next reception, the deep music of his accent will drift to her from afar, like waves upon an unimaginable Sicilian shore.

The dresser beyond the empty bed is white and bare. Everything is white. She has nothing to do. The gauze curtains make the room dim; beyond, the campus aches with green and blue, lacking her. She turns her head the other way. Her eyes burn.

She does not realize she has slept until the white room forms dimly around her once again. Someone is standing at her bedside. She looks up the narrow white dress past the antique brooch to the smiling face just out of focus. "Oh," she says. "Mrs. Hamilton."

From behind her back Mrs. Hamilton brings a dozen long-stemmed roses; their red is startling in the stark white room. "Oh," the girl says again. She cannot believe the dark sturdy leaves, the velvet blush of the petals, the cautionary finger at Mrs. Hamilton's lips.

The girl lies very still, waiting. From among the stems Mrs. Hamilton carefully draws a tiny white envelope and hands it to the girl. Her fingers are feverish upon the cool paper. It takes forever to pry open the flap, unfold the white card. Her burning eyes skip down the few words to find his name; her warm hands draw it to her flushed cheek.

If her vision were not too blurred surely she could at this moment foresee their return ten years hence to bring up their children in this college town. Surely she could see the white house where he and she will spend their lives, see the garden with peach trees, the downward slope toward burning sunsets which will draw at her heart the way red roses do, the way his name now does, held tightly against her hot face.

The Go-Between

She takes my younger brother and me down the walk. The narrow sections of concrete are uneven. The house is downhill from the brick street which runs along its front yard to the green and white campus and turns abruptly right. There is no board fence now, but on Sundays the girls still march to church in long files, two abreast, led and followed by sweet-faced chaperones.

It is a low white house. A faint voice has answered the knock: "Come on in." Inside it is so dark and musty that I clutch my mother's skirt. My brother wants to be held, but she moves him aside to get through the door. I am pulled behind her into a dark foyer, wide and bare; ahead it is shut off by a dark curtain.

"Back here." The voice is unbodied, ancient. My mother draws the curtain aside. Darker still. Someone in a chair, small, thin, straight. Her black dress comes all the way to the tips of black shoes. She wears a gray shawl. Her dark hair is pulled straight back. The air smells as if it has never stirred.

"How are you, Mrs. Hamilton?" my mother asks brightly. My brother and I are tight against her dress. Somewhere outside a mockingbird sings a clear, startling phrase, pauses, sings it again.

4 *There Is a Fountain*

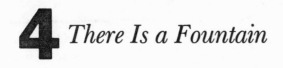

Francesca and I were born of the same blood in the same month, but by the time I arrive with my father in Palazzo Adriano, she and I have been separated by a generation, an ocean, the vast silence between Mississippi and Sicily for more than forty years. Her face is gentle, always a little distracted. Her mother's face sags heavily on one side from a recent stroke. Tetina, my cousin. She sits in the alcove, where a window is set into the thick stone walls, like a madonna in a shrine. The struggling lips are wet with tears and saliva when she tries to welcome my father, the Uncle Peppino who left for America before she was born, and me, the Cousin Roberto she didn't know existed.

Francesca has to do the talking; her voice is soft, tentative. She is very shy, and if I do not understand her murmured Sicilian immediately she shrugs in despair and her eyes dart to one of her daughters for help. Her husband is in the campagna tending to his cattle, goats, sheep, his olives, chestnuts, figs, pistachios, prickly pears; he makes cheese—good solid cacio—to send to America. Francesca is relieved when we have finished eating and she can say to my father and me, "Riposo, riposo," showing us into the shuttered room of her daughters. Outside, the sun is bright, the air clear and pure, the sky so deep a blue that you do not dare look into it for long.

She pats the bed of eleven-year-old Giuseppina for my father, that of four-year-old Carmeluccia for me. Tina, who is nine, giggles behind her hand because her bed is not to be occupied. "Riposo, riposo." Francesca backs out. Carmeluccia, against her mother's skirt, is like a painted doll. Tina's eyes are always bright: "Dormite bene," she says. The door closes on the cool darkness of midday.

My father begins snoring immediately. He is forty years older than I. I am forty years older than Carmeluccia. I sink into her bed. Eighty years ago, when my father was her age, this is where he would drop off to sleep, in this same little town of Palazzo Adriano. When I was her age, near Clinton, Mississippi, the sounds I would hear as sleep came on were the chickens clucking in our yard, my mother in the kitchen singing, "There is a fountain filled with blood. . . ." My mother had spent her childhood in Standing Pine, and some days as I would float out of consciousness, our chickens became those of my grandmother there on the farm, the cotton mattress became her deep feather bed, like this one of Carmeluccia's, and for a moment I would be where I was not, perhaps who I was not.

It is not chickens that I hear as my eyes close here in Carmeluccia's bed, and the voice which begins to sing somewhere near, as near as my mother's in the kitchen years ago, has in it none of the plank church and the slatted pew. It is as clear and pure, as cool and dark as the air in this shuttered childhood room. "Rose rosse per te. . . ." A single phrase, and then a slosh of water, the sound of scrubbing as with a brush. "Ho comprato stasera." I am cradled in the deep bed, safe; it becomes my own bed forty years ago; I become no older than Carmeluccia. The slosh of water, the scrubbing, the clear sweet phrases of the song—"D'amore non si muore"—are a rhythm like that of my blood, deep in me, and dark. The voice is that of my mother—the mother I might have had if my father had not left Sicily. I am the little Sicilian boy I might have been, coming out of sleep to the sound of her voice.

*   *   *

"Monello! Monello!" I am shaken, rolled, tumbled in the soft bed. "Bad boy! You want to sleep away your whole life?" I rub at my eyes and am lifted in my mother's arms; she is as full and soft as the bed. She laughs in my ear; her voice is always like music; it clears away the shadows of a dream I have been trying to keep in my head.

"Roberto! Vene cca!" It is my grandmother, calling from the other room. She sits all day in the chair, dark and short; her little arms can reach out and grab me no matter how far around her I try to pass, pull me to her to be examined, scolded, hugged. "Come kiss your nanna good morning. It is a beautiful day, a very special day. . . ." Her voice chokes. She begins to cry. "Oh," she is wailing. "Oh, San Giuseppe be praised. . . ."

"Mamma, mamma," my mother says. "He does not understand."

"Sò papà," my grandmother cries. "He will get to see his father at last. He will not remember him."

My mother laughs again and kisses my ear loudly. "He is a very clever boy, but not that clever." She holds me out from her, shakes me. "My little genius," she says, "do you remember the day they took your father away? Of course you do! You were a grown young man, already a year old. And your Uncle Carmeluccio? And your cousins, Sebastiano and Nino? Do you remember when you used to kick me in the belly from the inside? Il risorgimento—remember that, more than half a century ago? Garibaldi let you ride his horse, remember?"

"Rosa!" My grandmother cries out. "You'll have his brains all scrambled. He'll grow up to be a madman."

I laugh because my mother is laughing. In the festa the men raced mules up the street into the piazzetta below Garibaldi and one of them hit the sack with his stick and got ashes all in his face, and everybody laughed. It was a trick, my mother said; sometimes the winner got a chicken all plucked and ready to cook. "I'm hungry," I tell my mother.

"Well, get dressed and come on." When she puts me down, the tile floor is cold to my bare feet. "I'll stuff you like a goose."

"Rosa! For shame!" My grandmother begins crying again. "He should have gone to America with the others, your Peppino. His brother Giorgio is a very rich man, and his Tony is known all around the world. The fascisti cannot touch them there. Nobody put Giorgio in prison for three years away from his children. His Giuseppina did not kill herself with hard work and heartbreak while the fascisti tried to take his land."

She is still crying when we go into the room, but her short arms reach me all the same and I am smothered to her; her wet face is against my forehead. "Ah, Roberto. You do not remember Garibaldi, pay no attention to your mother; but never forget Mussolini. It is his men who killed your father's sister. Her husband and her sons and her brother all in prison, what was she to do? She rode a horse like a man, but it was too much for her. Her heart could not stand it. And now they come home to find that she is dead. Feliciuzza, Feliciuzza, sister of my daughter's husband, you were like flesh and blood to me."

I am being rocked from side to side; it is hard to breathe, but I know not to pull away from my grandmother. I am not sure what she is talking about, but she is crying. "Nanna, nanna," I say as well as I can with my face pressed so out of shape.

"Come on, Goose. Turkey. Rooster. We'll stuff your craw." My mother pulls me away and pushes me ahead of her to the kitchen. The sticks are burning under the coffee, and it goes up into the top of the pot with a sound like the water below my grandfather's mill wheel. "Just in time." She moves the pot off the fire. The smell seems to bring all the daylight into my head. I watch my mother pour the dark coffee into two cups, spoon sugar in, stir. She looks at me and laughs. "Tomorrow there will be three, and still none for you."

"I want a taste," I tell her.

"Monello! You want everything." She holds out the cup, as she does every morning. "All right. Just a sip."

I let the thick coffee touch my lip; it is sweet and strong.

Francesca plays without talking, except to herself. She sits near the wall in the wooden chair her father brought her from Palermo. The sun is warm on her there, I hear her telling herself. Her cheeks look as if they have been painted on, I have heard my mother say, and her eyes, watching me always though always turned away, are large and brown. I tell her that Garibaldi let me ride his horse and I rode faster than anybody into the piazzetta, and hit the sack with my stick and got ashes in my face. I stagger around, brushing wildly at the dry ashes, and when I hear her laugh I do it again. The white chicken flaps its wings, getting out of my way, and then squawks and runs farther down the cobblestone street, away from a man who has come up the stone steps beside the house. I chase the chicken, shouting, "Gaddina! I will tear out your feathers and cook you in a pot."

The man has stopped, and he speaks to Francesca. "Come ti chiami, pretty little girl?"

Francesca looks away. "She is Francesa," I say. "She doesn't like to talk."

"Buccola," the man says. "Francesca Buccola."

Francesca's head moves up and down once, so little that you can hardly tell it. She does not look at the man.

"And you, with the blue eyes, what's your name?" He stoops down to look me in the face, and I can see that his eyes are blue too. I forget for the moment that he has asked me who I am. "Roberto, non è vero?" His hand is out as though he will draw me to him. "Roberto Canzoneri, son of Peppino who has been away?" I nod, scarcely more than Francesca. He clears his throat. "They said you would be here. I am your father." His arms come around me and I am against the strange face, rough, like my grandfather's. I do not know what I am supposed to do, and I stand rigidly against him. "Figlio mio, figlio

mio," he is saying. "My son, my son." He smells like my grandfather, too, and when I hug him as I would my grandfather,
his face stiffens against mine. Behind me, Francesca's chair is
scraping across the cobblestones, and I can hear her telling
herself that she must sit in the shade or the sun will cook her
brains, just as I have heard her mother say it.

Something has stirred me. I hear the early cluck of a hen outside in the street. A mule is clop-clopping on the cobblestones,
going away. Someone is riding out to the campagna; I will
hear him coming back before dark. I imagine I can hear the
soft pat of goat's feet following along behind, but when I
strain my ears all I hear is a vendor's cry, far off in the town
somewhere: "Milanggiani!" He will pass in front of our house
later, walking beside the cart full of dark eggplants.

"Roberto." It is a man's voice, not my mother's. I open my
eyes. It is my father. He must have been standing over me,
waiting. "Figlio mio, you want to get up? It is morning."

"Mamma," I say.

He turns toward the door, bites his lip. I am watching him.
"Rosa," he says. "He wants you."

My mother comes in, but she does not tumble me. She takes
my father's arm. "He'll get used to you," she says. "Be patient."
Suddenly she pounces on me and rolls me over in the bed.
"Monello! You are naughty even in your dreams. Why did you
dream about pinching Francesca so hard? What do you mean
running away so we have to dream that we search and search
for you and wake up already tired?" She rubs my face in the
pillow. "Monello! You get worse every night." She jerks me up
and holds me as if I am trying to escape. I put my arms
around her neck so tightly no one can take me away.

My father laughs. "You're going to make him tough."

"That's the only way to wake him up," my mother says. "You
have to start his blood rushing through his body."

"I wanted him to go to the mill with me."

"He'll go. But wait until he has eaten. He's worthless till then." She digs her finger into my side until I squirm. "There's nothing to him. We have to stuff his skin with straw to find out where he is."

My grandmother cries out from the next room as if in pain. "Rosa! What will your husband think? She does not feed him straw, like an animal, Peppineddu, but she does stuff his head with nonsense."

My father laughs quietly, looking at my mother. "I think he's a little goat." He takes something from his pocket—a key, a coin, a little knife?—looks at it, puts it back.

My mother touches him again. "Come along," she says. "The coffee will be ready." I close my eyes tightly until she sets me down in the kitchen.

He swallows his coffee in one gulp and watches me taste my mother's. Suddenly he hunches his shoulders. "I can't wait," he says.

My mother smiles at him. "Peppe, Peppe. You go on. I'll bring him to the mill."

"No," he says. "No. I want to walk with him. I'll wait in the piazzetta, at the foot of the steps."

I can hear the faint smack-smack as he kisses my grandmother on each cheek. "Ci videmmu, mia sòggira."

"Peppineddu, Peppineddu. You are the husband of my daughter, but you are a son to me as you were to your poor dead sister. When your mother died, who comforted you? Feliciuzza. Now she is gone."

"Basta," my father is saying softly. "That's enough, madre mia."

She is still weeping so when my mother takes me out that I think she will not see me, but at once I am smothered in the black dress all wet with tears. "Roberto, niputeddu. Now your father is home you will forget all about your nanna."

As we are walking through the piàzza, my father is stopped by an old man who embraces him, crying, "Peppino, you are home!" I stand by the fountain, watching the long-haired sheep drink. The water spouting from the lion's mouth is very cold. I let it run over my finger until it is numb. My father is telling the old man, yes, it was very hard, being in prison for nothing, no charges ever brought. They thought it would be impossible to keep the land producing, with the men away, and it could be taken for the taxes, but Feliciuzza kept up the work herself, with the help of only two farmhands. That was what killed her.

I have heard it all before, last night, with everybody crowded into my grandfather's house. Francesca got down off her mother's lap and disappeared under the table, and when I bent down she was looking through all the legs at me. I turned down my lips and wagged my head the way her grandfather did when he was talking, and she put her hand over her mouth and turned away, still watching me. Her grandfather was saying that they were not even allowed to talk to each other, and so they learned to talk with their hands like deaf people. I stood up to see, and my father's fingers were going fast, and suddenly the one called Sebastiano laughed. "It is true, Peppino," he said. "The wine bottles need to be filled again."

My grandfather laughed too. He said that he would never forget when Peppineddu was no bigger than Roberto here, at the wedding of Feliciuzza, may the Blessed Virgin watch over her soul, and Carmeluccio, praise be to Mary, returned home at last. Little Peppineddu drank too much wine and tried to fly off the steps of the Greek church.

From the fountain I can see the curved steps of the Greek church, where Francesca goes, and the square steps of the Latin church, where my mother takes me sometimes. My father was no bigger than I am when he tried to fly. I try to imagine him so, but I cannot make his face look any different from now. He becomes a small boy with a big man's head. He leaps off the steps and flies across the piazza toward me. Before I know it I have run to my father; I am standing close beside him. He stops talking to the old man and looks down at me. For the first time I see him smile, and his face is not the scary one on the flying boy. "You are right, Roberto," he says. "We have stopped here too long."

He is helping my grandfather clean the millstone; I can hear them talking through the sound of water below the wheel. I put dry leaves in the water and watch them twist away.

"But you just got home!" my grandfather is saying. "Are you crazy? You want to leave your wife and son already?"

"What is there to do here? I will work in America and I will send for them."

"You can work with me in the mill, as before."

"It brings in only enough for you and my stepmother. You have starved yourselves to feed Rosa and Roberto while I was gone."

"No, no. We have not starved. Do I look like a man who has starved?"

For a while there is only the scraping sound, the water curling around my hand. "I have to go," my father says finally. "I will write Giorgio to lend me my passage, and he will help me find work there."

Once more it is quiet. I break a shiny green fig leaf off the tree. I lay it carefully on the water, feel it pull, let go. The leaf turns over slowly. I can see round drops of water riding its underside as it goes out of sight.

"Then we are safe," my grandfather says. "When in all your life have you ever written a letter to anyone?"

"You talk as if I can't write, when I taught myself right here under your nose. Didn't I learn to keep records for you, even though you took me out of school?"

"Well, what was I to do? If the teacher had beaten you one more time, I would have killed him."

"I know, papà."

The pen and paper and inkwell have been on the table for days. They draw me to them, but I am not allowed to touch them. Once I picked up the pen, but my mother yelled at me from the kitchen so sharply that I jumped. "No, no, Roberto," she said, wiping her hands on her apron as she came to me. "You must not. Leave the paper alone." Her hands were still damp when she put them on my cheeks and looked me in the eyes. "Promise?"

I nodded. "Promise."

It took her a moment to smile. "What were you going to do? Write the story of your life in three sentences?"

"I was going to make a picture."

"Of what?"

I shrugged my shoulders. It had been something, a line that would have become something. A mountain? A cow? The peach tree in my grandfather's garden? Whatever it had been, it was gone.

"I know," she said. "You were going to draw every single person in Palazzo, with heads no bigger than the point of a pin, and all the eyes and noses and mouths exactly right. 'Look,' people would say, 'there is Francesca, and her mother, Tetina. See? It is just like them! And the old man who sweeps the piazza, and the priest at the Greek church with the funny beard. Meraviglioso!' And everyone who saw it would be so fascinated they could not stop looking until every tiny face had been named, and they would all go blind with eyestrain." She grabbed me up and held me tightly to her, swinging from side to side. "Monello! I knew you were up to some mischief."

Sometimes my father sits at the table and holds the pen, staring at the paper. Then he will get up and walk around and sit down again. "We do not want you to go anyway," my mother has said once. And another time, "Such a letter is very difficult, Peppe."

Tonight he stands up suddenly and shouts, "What is the matter with me? When I sit down to write, all the blood goes out of my head and everything is as blank as the paper. My hands sweat. My heart beats so loudly it rings in my ears."

"Perhaps your heart does not want you to go away."

He turns to my mother. "I can write. You have seen me."

"Of course you can write. But how do you go about writing the brother you have not seen for thirty years? It is not like writing the kilos of wheat ground for la Signora Gallo to make bread."

"You think I cannot do it. You hope I will never get the letter written."

"I don't want you to go, that is true."

"You see? How can I write when you are working so against me?"

She lays her hands on his arm. "Peppe, my Peppe. It is your decision. You have decided. I cannot want you to go, but I will help you if I can."

He sits down again, leans back with his hand on his forehead. "There is no way you can help."

"You believe I do not want to help."

He does not look at her. I am in my grandmother's lap, being rocked back and forth as though nothing is happening. I keep expecting her hand to cover my mouth, even though I will not try to say anything. The last time my mother and father were talking about the letter, I opened my mouth and my mother looked at me hard and said, "Silenziu," in a voice like stone.

"You see?" my mother cries. "You see? You want to believe that I am against you! You want to hate me for it!" She rushes to the table and takes the paper. "Here. I will prove to you that you are wrong." She picks up the pen, but he grabs it too. "There is only one way not to go through life hated by my husband," she says. "I must write the letter."

"I can write it!"

"Of course you can write it. And you can go off to America with bitterness, believing your Rosa tried to tie you down."

"Isn't it true?"

"Peppe, please. If I write on one sheet of paper, will that keep you from writing on another? Send whatever you choose, but let me write a letter, only to take the suspicion from your heart."

Slowly he lets her take the pen from his hand. "If that is the reason."

She sits, thinks for a moment, dips the pen into the ink, begins scratching on the paper. He stands and watches, puts his hand on her shoulder. "You write with beautiful strokes," he says.

She looks up at him and smiles. I cannot see his face, but when I think she is going to turn back to the writing, she does not, and suddenly they are both laughing. He takes her head in his arms.

"Now," my grandmother whispers to me, pushing me off her lap, but I do not know how to get between them.

He is gasping with laughter. "'Mio caro fratello Giorgio,'" he manages to say. "My dear brother Giorgio. Why couldn't I have thought of that?"

My father picks up the letter very carefully. "Come, Roberto," he says.

"Don't drop it, Peppe," my mother tells him. "If it shatters Giorgio may not be able to piece it together."

I take my father's hand. "Go with him, Roberto," my grandmother is saying, as if I am not on my way. "Soon he will leave again, and it will be a long time before you go to him, far off in a strange land." I stay on the other side of my father from her. "Life is hard," she says, "and not even il Papa goes straight to heaven."

Francesca does not look our way as we approach her house. She is on the doorstep, tapping a long wooden spoon on the stone, very softly. "Bon giorno," my father says to her. "Comu si?"

She keeps her eyes on the spoon. Her mouth forms a word and she breathes it out into the cool morning air. "Bona."

"E to' mamma. Tetina? to' papà?"

"Boni."

"We're going to the post office," I tell her. "And then we will go to America and live there forever."

The brown eyes turn enough for me to see them. The spoon hesitates. Then she looks down and the tapping begins again.

A mule is drinking where Francesca's mother gets water, and we go wide around so his heels cannot reach us. Water never stops splashing in the basin except when Tetina holds a jar under the spout and the sound becomes smooth and dark. You can tell from listening when it is full, and when she lets you look inside you can see the bottom of the jar through your own eyes looking back at you. "Will Francesca go to America too?" I ask my father.

"No. But your Uncle Ciro has a daughter you can play with in New York."

The street widens into the piazzetta Garibaldi. "This is where the mules ran," I tell him.

He stops and looks all around. The piazzetta is empty. "Once I stopped to watch them here," he says, "and forgot I was supposed to be delivering flour. My father grabbed me from behind, like this." He takes me by the shoulders. "And he picked me up and set me on my donkey." He sets me on an imaginary donkey, laughs, puts me down. "He is a strong man, you know. I was bigger than you are, ten or eleven years old."

Suddenly he points across to a door. "That's where I started to school and the teacher beat me with a cane. Knocked me down and beat me. I tried to fight back, but he was a man and I was a boy." He takes my hand again and we walk across the piazzetta. "My father started after him with a gun. . . ."

He is silent as we pass under an old woman leaning from her balcony, her eyes following us all the way. Then he says, "You will go to school in America. They will not beat you there." His hand tightens on mine. "I won't let them."

The man in the post office motions my father to the last window, and I can hear him saying, "It was a crime. They are wolves. They are vultures. Maybe it will get better, maybe worse." He takes the letter, examines it on both sides, puts stamps on it, tosses it into a box.

My father's eyes do not leave the letter. "How long will it take?"

The man shrugs his shoulders. "Who knows, Peppe? Tomorrow it will go to Palermo. Before many days a ship will leave for New York, but with how many ports on the way? Maybe a month to reach your brother."

"A month?"

"Two or three months before you get his letter in return, if he is in a hurry to reply."

Out in the street my father looks up at the sky. The clouds are gray and ragged and they move fast. He takes my hand and starts walking, but not toward home. The street curves and climbs out of town toward Monte Rose. My legs get very tired. When I stumble, my father lifts me high and sets me on his shoulders. I hold onto his head and he is holding my feet so that I will not fall backward. "I am your donkey," he says.

We climb and climb. Sometimes he carries me and sometimes I walk alongside the path of crushed rock. He tells me he used to walk this trail every week, all the way up and around Monte Rose to Bivona, where his father had a mill for a while, carrying fresh bread and clean clothes. He tells me how my mother used to smile at him from her balcony, and his father was afraid they would run away and get married, but they didn't. Money was so scarce that they waited a long time.

He stops and looks back at the town, and I look too. We are high above the red tile roofs. Far off on another mountain there is another town, as gray and high as the clouds. "Prizzi," my father says. "My family came from there." He picks me up and sets me on a big rock. The clouds are rushing overhead so close that I am afraid they will brush my face. The wind is strong and cold, and it makes the whole valley look wild. "I used to back up to this rock and rest my pack on it." My father backs up to me now. "Get on. We'll pretend you are just a bundle of clothes and bread."

A tall thin lady is talking to my father. "Ah, you see?" she says. My father has been rubbing the flour between his thumb and finger, looking out the back of the mill toward the Church of the Madonna delle Grazie, as if listening. The millstone is turning fast. He has handed the lady a pinch of the flour, which she is feeling too. "Your father is a good miller, Peppino but since you were a boy only you could grind wheat for me to just the right fineness. I am happy you are home at last."

My father laughs. "I was afraid I might have forgotten, but the memory is still in my fingers."

She touches her tongue to the flour. "When I have made the bread, I will take it to the furnu myself and eat the first piece hot with olive oil."

My father looks at me. "Does that make you hungry, Roberto? Here." He gives me some flour warm from the mill. I lick it a little at a time. When I have finished, he rubs his handkerchief around my mouth and brushes off my hand. "Anyone could tell by looking you are the son of a miller."

My grandfather has come in. "The son and grandson," he says. When the lady has left with her flour, he turns to my father. "I had hoped he might work with you here as you have worked with me."

My father is silent for a moment. "You know what they say. Mussolini will build power plants and you will be put out of business by electricity. And the flour will be . . ." He looks as if he will spit, " . . . nenti."

My grandfather leans in the stone doorway, looking out at the church high up the hill beyond the vineyards, at the cemetery black with cypresses. "We are living in a strange time, Peppino. The earth itself shifts under our feet."

"Come warm yourself, Roberto. Quickly! The cold will make your bones ache." I throw the covers off and run into the other room toward the brazier. "Not too close! You'll burn yourself!" My grandmother has me. The sound of rain that kept me under the surface of sleep is very clear now. I can hear the hard drip-drip off the roof onto the stone beyond the door. And the voices: "He does not answer because he does not want me there."

"Now, Peppe."

"Why should he bother to write a letter? He is so far away who can call him to account?"

"Giorgio is not that kind of man, Peppe. He will answer."

"He will say that he has no money."

"I do not understand what has happened," my mother says. They are having their coffee in the kitchen, and I did not get my taste. "Don't expect me to understand."

"It is the Exchange that failed. But my brother has land, and my nephew Tony is champion of the world. If he says they have no money to lend me, it is a lie."

My mother's voice is hesitant. " I do not know, Peppe. They say men who were very rich have been leaping from skyscrapers."

The coals are ashen, but I can feel the warmth on my hands and face. I am leaning against my grandmother's little arms as if they were a stone balustrade. "I want my coffee," I say.

"Shhh," my grandmother says in my ear. "Patience."

"Ah," my father says. "Who knows? The men who got rich in the Exchange did not understand it, or they would not be sprawled dead on the city streets. Who am I to talk about it?"

"I didn't get my coffee," I say again.

My mother comes into the room, holds her hands over the brazier, looks toward the hard drip-drip beyond the door. "You were a sleepyhead," she says after a moment. Then she looks at me, comes around the brazier and pinches my arm. "Are you awake yet? As long as you are dreaming anyway, why don't you dream your sip of coffee?" She takes me from my grandmother. "Monello! Greedy boy! I will roast your feet in the fire. What do you mean dreaming up a whole pot just for yourself?"

Over her shoulder I can see my father in the kitchen. He picks up something and comes to me. "Here, Roberto," he says, holding out the little coffee cup. "Touch your tongue to that." In the bottom the sugar is thick and black, as sweet as candy, and cold.

The white speck lands on my nose. It makes a spot of cold so tiny I turn myself cross-eyed trying to see it.

"Snow," my father says. "Some years it will cover the ground and everything will be white."

Another speck floats down not far away. I run after it. My father laughs. "Rosa," he calls. "Come out here."

The flakes begin coming in clouds. We run together, sticking out our tongues to catch them. Francesca is standing outside her house with her mother.

Tetina waves her arm. "Bella!" she cries. Francesca is tight against her, her hand held out very still to let the flakes touch down and melt.

"I wish it would fill the streets clear up to the rooftops," my mother says.

Through the snow I can see a man coming, faint as a ghost. I cannot tell it is my cousin Nino until he is right upon us. "You like this, Roberto?" he asks me. "If it snows enough, I will make a sled for you and Francesca." Nino is very strong, and there is a scar on his arm where a bullet went through in the Great War; the sleeve of his coat covers it now. He is handing my father something. "I was at the post office," he says. "Your letter came."

My father holds the letter in both hands. Snow keeps falling into his dark hair like bits of flour. "It is for me?"

My mother laughs. "It is for Pio the Eleventh, but you wanted a letter so badly he sent you one of his."

My father is still looking at the envelope as if he cannot see it clearly through the snow. "Is it from Giorgio?" He puts his finger on the corner and reads, "G. Canzoneri. Marlboro, N.Y. U.S.A."

"Open it, Peppe," my mother says.

"Come inside and read it," Tetina tells him. "The melting flakes will make the ink run."

My father does not move. The snow has been swirling around him, but now that the wind has stopped it settles through the air very slowly. I watch Francesca's hand; it looks as if it is floating upward to meet the slow flakes.

"I can't," my father says. "It will be full of excuses, and I do not want to hate my brother."

My mother touches his face. "My Peppe. I will read it first." He does not give the letter to her, but when she takes it from his hands he says nothing.

Tetina moves toward the door. "Don't you want to come inside?" They do not seem to hear her.

My mother tears open the envelope very carefully, unfolds the letter, looks at it for a moment. She clears her throat. " 'It is with great joy that I receive the news that you are free at last and will come to America.' "

My father is staring at her. "He says that?"

She nods. Her face looks for a moment as though the cold has frozen it. She puts her fingers into the envelope, tries to see in, draws out another piece of paper. "He sent an order for the money to pay for your passage."

"Giorgio," my father says. Nino puts his hand on his shoulder.

My mother reads silently again; her eyes move swiftly. "He says that times are very bad and there are no jobs, but he does not think he will lose the farm. Ciro works as a butcher in another city not far away. Vincenzina's husband has work nearby, nobody knows for how long. Ninfa and her husband have the strawberry farm in Louisiana, but he thinks they will come live near him. He says, 'You can work on the farm and help in the hotel. There will be plenty to eat and plenty of wine, although it is difficult to get money. No one knows how long it will be this way.' "

Nino is holding my father's shoulder. "You will go to America," he says.

Tetina begins to cry. She kisses my father loudly on each side of his face. "Zio Peppino," she says. "You have just come back to us and you will go away never to return."

My mother's hands are unsteady as she folds the letter and puts it back into the envelope. The snow no longer floats down; it has become round and hard. I watch a piece strike Francesca's pale fingers, sit there as solid and white as a chip of marble, and then turn to nothing. Out of the corner of her eye, she is watching me. Carefully, as though the moisture on her palm might spill, she moves her hand down to her wool skirt and wipes it dry. Tetina is crying. "Come inside. You must come into my house. Do not insult me by refusing."

The Blessed Virgin is smiling down at me from a picture on the wall. Her heart is outside where I can see it, red as blood. It begins swelling, and her face grows fat and ugly. She opens her great yellow mouth and there are long teeth ready to bite me. "Mamma!" I hear myself screaming. "Mamma!"

I feel the soft hands on my face, feel them begin to lift me before my eyes will come open. The picture is back on the wall over my bed. The face, dim in the faint light, is smiling, but I bury my own face in my mother's shoulder. Who knows when it will change again?

"It's all right, Roberto. It's all right. Did you have a bad dream?"

My father has come into my room. He puts his hand on my neck, moves my head gently around, feels my forehead. "He has a fever," he says. "I'll make a fire and go get my father."

The fire blazes in the brazier. I am warm, held tightly by my mother. The inkwell makes a short leaping shadow on the wall beyond the table. It has been there for days, again, but my father will not let my mother write the letter. "I can do it," he said when he put out the pen and paper. "It's very simple. 'Mio caro fratello Giorgio.'"

My mother sings to me in a low voice. "Fammi sognar. . . ." My grandmother has been staying with her sick brother in Chiusa Sclafani, and she is supposed to come home today. I begin to go to sleep, but the shadow of the inkwell turns into a huge black bird which blots out the firelight, and I pull myself awake. "Roberto," my mother is saying. "It's all right."

When my father returns with my grandfather, the coals in the brazier are red. My grandfather takes off his heavy coat and makes a face at me. "Let me see the little rascal," he says. "Pretending to be sick, is he? He's just a fannullone trying to get out of work." His hand on my forehead is not soft like my mother's, but it has the gentle touch of my father's. He feels my neck on the sides and under my chin, pulls up my shirt and presses his fingers around over my stomach. It makes me giggle. "You see? He's not sick at all." He pulls my shirt back down. "I'll make him a tea to drink, and tomorrow he'll eat a cartload of pasta."

"I'm sorry we woke you early," my mother says. "Stay while I make coffee."

My grandfather nods. "But it isn't early for me. I had been up half an hour when Peppino came for me."

My mother hands me to my father and goes to the kitchen. She stops in the door and turns back to the table. "What is this?"

My father sits in my grandmother's chair, stroking my arm. "Last night. After you fell asleep. I didn't want. . . ."

She is breathing hard. Now she holds the paper aside to get the light from the coals. She reads silently, shakes her head once, reads again. "Peppe," she says.

My father's hand is still stroking my arm. "Read it aloud," he says. "My father does not believe I can write a letter."

" 'Mio caro fratello Giorgio,' " my mother says, and begins laughing so that she cannot read. My father laughs too, but quietly, as though waiting. "I'm sorry," she says. "Here, I'll read the letter." She clears her throat, makes her face straight, and begins again. " 'My dear brother Giorgio, I thank you with all my heart. I am returning the order for money. I cannot come. With affection, your brother, Peppino.' " Her voice is becoming smothered before she finishes, and then she collapses in laughter, hugs my father and me so tightly that I cannot breathe.

My grandfather clears his throat. "You are going to stay, Peppino?"

I can feel my father trying to nod his head. Suddenly he is laughing hard too. "It seemed . . ." he says, and then gets a breath. "It seemed like a long letter, last night."

My mother lets us go and stands over us for a moment, no longer laughing. "Why, Peppe? Why can't you go?"

He shakes his head. "I would go and eat Giorgio's food and drink his wine, but how long before I could get money to repay him? How long before I could get passage for my . . . ?" His voice stops. He is holding me so tightly that I could not move if I wanted to.

"Make the coffee, Rosa," my grandfather says.

"I want some," I say.

My grandfather takes me from my father, turns his mouth down at the corners, and growls at me, "No coffee, Roberto. Not until you are well." I twist in his arms. My father is still sitting in my grandmother's chair. My mother puts the letter slowly on the table.

"I will add a few words, Peppe, if you want me to."

"That would be good." He shakes his head slowly. "I worked at it half the night." His eyes do not leave her. I watch her too as she goes into the kitchen, watch her through the doorway. I hold my eyes wide. The shadow of the inkwell is not there any more, but I am afraid that if I begin to fall asleep it will return and blot out all that I see.

* * *

Supper is over. Francesca's husband is home from the campagna, and our relatives have gathered two or three at a time: Nino's wife, Marietta, and their daughters, Felicina and Giovanna. Sebastiano's widow, Antonietta, and daughter, Felicina, in black. Giuseppina and Tina and Pippo. Nino and three Carmelos and perhaps Nicola and Anna will come later; the talk—the attempt to talk—is too much for them to take for a whole evening.

I am tired myself. Speaking Italian without knowing it is exhausting. Seeing Tetina at the other end of the table, warped, unable to speak at all, depresses me. I watch the children.

Carmeluccia is playing by herself near her mother's feet. Tina brings me drawings done in school and Giuseppina hands me an essay; I can make out enough to know that the style is very formal, perhaps elegant. "Buono," I say. "Molto brava."

My father is telling silent Tetina, in English, about an incident in a Mississippi Baptist church where he preached. Francesca's sister-in-law has come in with her two small daughters. They are visitors here in Palazzo, too, from Rome. Patricia clings to her mother's knees. Roberta, a chubby five-year-old, constantly circles about as if to some private tune. I feel that I am on the verge of understanding the bright conversations she carries on in three voices. She will not look directly at me, moves in arcs well out of my reach. Abruptly she stops playing, holds her arms out wide, runs to me. I lean down to let her hug my neck. Then she draws back and whispers to Giovanna, "È sette kilometri lungo."

I am seven kilometers long. For the first time I realize that I am nearly a foot taller than my cousins here, I am bearded, I am wearing a yellow sport coat. I look around the table, and everyone except Tetina smiles without speaking. No one is ready yet for the evening's struggle to tell each other what it is like to be different.

5 Standing Pine

She would hurry toward us down sandstone slabs between square-trimmed boxwoods, arms wide, crying out our names. We would scramble out of the Model A and run to be enfolded. The wide apron is heavy with flour; I bury my face in it, arms as far around her as I can get them.

My grandmother—the only one I knew—at the house in Standing Pine. Always in my memory I am at apron level, but the flour dusted on that apron is from ginger snaps she mailed wherever I was during the war. Ungainly packages addressed in her unmistakable hand, brown wrapping paper dark in splotches where the shortening soaked through. Thick doughy cookies without much snap, every batch a little different because she measured by hand and eye.

Tessie Devona Matheny, wife of Arden Margrave Barnett, had a cast-iron opinion about everything. Hers was the central position in the universe and she kept hauling people to it: Shake a leg! she would cry to those behind her; Make haste! To those off on a tangent she called, Hold on; hold on there! half in the hope that they would square off and argue.

She must have been in her seventies when I sat one day by the bed in which she lay pale and listless. While I was groping for some way to cheer her up, a man dropped in and said,

"Maybe you don't remember me, Miss Tessie, but I carved the tombstone for Ďr. Arden back in 1932."

"Oh?" she said weakly.

"I'm not here on business," he assured her. "It was a double headstone. I was just visiting my folks up the road and heard you were sick, and I thought I'd come see how you are." He leaned forward in his chair. "How are you?"

She moved hardly enough to reply. "Oh, I've just about give up."

"No, no, Miss Tessie," he said. "You can't do that."

She sat fulľ up in bed and glared at him. "Why can't I?" she demanded. "Give me one good reason!"

Perhaps a dozen years later she was visited by some people who had been tracing out the Matheny family in the United States.

"Well, yes," my grandmother said, "Arden's family was English, but we're Scotch-Irish."

"No," the people said. "You're French."

She sat without rocking for a moment. Then she said, "And I've never liked the French."

It is tempting to imagine that she put up the argument of her life when my mother, at twenty, decided to marry an older man, a Sicilian with a heavy accent, but my mother says there was no opposition, and from the time I can remember my grandmother and my father got along beautifully.

My grandfather, who was a preacher as well as a doctor and a farmer, refused to officiate at the wedding, but he refused to officiate at her brothers', too. I remember him as a tall slender man; I see him on the roadside, speaking to my father and me in a courtly fashion, as though we were strangers at some august event; sitting quietly in the front room, reading by the yellow light of the kerosene lamp; laid out on the daybed gaunt and still, with coins on his eyes. I have been told that he was a melancholy man; certainly the bits of his poetry I have seen are in the melancholy tone of Tennyson that seems to have appealed to many Southern gentlemen.

Whatever discussion he and my grandmother may have had about their daughter's marriage to a foreigner, they could easily have listed a number of things in his favor: He was, after all, a Baptist minister, a graduate of Mississippi College, and one of his "Fathers in Christ," Old Brother Moore, was the local pastor and a highly respected friend. No one who had been swept up in the gospel songs that he led could doubt that he was bound for the promised land. Dishonorable intentions could never have hidden behind those open blue eyes and that expressive face. Besides, it was the English and the French my grandmother never liked, and if it was only the Germans I recall her admiring, I never heard her say anything against the Italians.

Sometimes my father was along and sometimes he was away in a revival meeting when we visited Standing Pine; sometimes it was just us, and sometimes my mother's brothers and their wives and children would gather at the same time. Uncle Arden would be dressed in a neat suit and tie; he would sit quietly, smoking a good cigar, smiling slightly as Uncle Tracy, in shirtsleeves, settled his six-feet-four on its backbone deep in a chair, and from down behind his knees took in half the room with his arms, describing a fish he'd caught. Or, "EeeeNORmous big snake," he'd say, eyes wild above his glasses. "Stretch from that settee to that wall over yonder. Big around as my thigh. I may be getting a few years on me, and I had on those heavy fishing boots, but I just climbed up and stood there patting the air with my feet like a sparrow hawk till he crawled out from under me." Whatever he said, Uncle Chester would dust the eternal ash from his cigarette and counter, "No. That ain't so."

We kids would swing on the grapevines at the back of the pasture, play cars with Prince Albert cans in the sand of the mule wallow, slide in our Sunday clothes down the wet sides of red clay gullies and get simultaneous spankings. Some of us would sleep in feather beds, buried up to our noses; others would be on pallets on the wooden floor, watching pine chunks in the fireplace go from a scorching blaze to sifting coals to darkness.

On each first Sunday in August not only my mother's immediate family, but the entire clan gathered around long tables on the hard-packed yard or under oak trees up at my Great-uncle Oscar's for the Barnett reunion. Before we expected it, my generation found ourselves the uncles and aunts, and even though we've edged over now into great-uncles and -aunts, I suppose the reunion will always seem most real to us as it was when we were the kids. For me, the events of all those gatherings during the thirties have coalesced into the reunion of 1933 when I was "the boy" who ran away, and certain relatives, including my brothers as I then perceived them, have been reduced to such essences that I have felt obliged to give them different names.

Reunion

"The blood from Barnett veins has flowed, my friends, for freedom. My—ah—kinfolks and—ah—relatives. My fellow Barnetts—ah—by whatever name. For we all have Barnett blood, my friends, or we wouldn't be gathered here today."

The boy's name was not Barnett. His father had come here from Sicily a long time ago. He squirmed against his mother. "When are we going?" he whispered.

"Hush up," his grandmother said. "Hush up and listen. Your Cousin Orford is making a speech."

"And I say to you that the blood we have in our veins has been shed—ah—Cousin Lester, for freedom, and it has been soaked into the soil of France, and into the crest—ah—of San Juan Hill—you know about that, Uncle Jess, lost a boy there in '98—and not to mention—ah—the sacred soil of our beloved Southland, where my daddy, and you—ah—Uncle Oscar, and—ah—others I'm sure, fought to the death—ah—though the Lord saw fit to spare them—for the purity of our race, and—ah—our—ah—our very blood."

"How long is he going to talk?" the boy asked. It was Sunday. His father was away in a revival that ended with the morning service. They'd meet him at the depot when they drove back through Jackson. "When are we going?"

"You'll wake up your brother," his grandmother said.

His mother leaned toward him. "After a while," she said quietly. Billy was asleep, his head in her lap.

Cousin Orford was tall and thin. He wore a dark coat, though most of the men were in shirtsleeves, and sweat had soaked big patches down its sides. Every year he made a speech at the reunion. He was running for office, people said. Some of them laughed about it.

The boy saw Truett sneaking toward the barn. Truett was his first cousin, younger than he was, but only by a few months. He did things like getting eggs from the nests and making corn bread—egg bread, he called it—out of the fresh eggs and mud, until Aunt Alice caught him. He had an old muffin pan behind the cow shed to make the bread in. Truett motioned the boy to come with him.

The boy pulled his mother's head down. "I'm going to where Truett is," he said.

"Shush," his grandmother said. "It's not polite to whisper."

"All right," his mother said. "But y'all behave."

He went behind the people as though toward Aunt Alice; if they had known Truett wasn't with her, they might not have let him go. Then he stepped quietly into the bright sunlight. All his relatives were under the oak trees, sitting in straight chairs on bare packed dirt. "Strothers Funeral Parlor lent 'em to us. They're awful nice, there." He had heard some aunt or cousin say that. The oak leaves were dusty and tough. In the midst of the relatives, his Great-uncle Oscar sat tall and straight facing his Second Cousin Orford. It was Uncle Oscar's house they were in front of, a wide house with a gallery across the front and halfway around one side. There was no railing, only a few thin posts from the edge of the porch to the edge of the roof. At the side was the washstand with a bucket of well water, beneath a tin dipper hanging on a nail. Children were not allowed on the gallery at reunion time—there were too many of them—but once when just his family was there the boy had been given a drink; the thin metal dipper was as cold as the water; it had been touched by the lips of great-uncles and great-aunts, of cousins old and young.

Clouds

From the barn he looked back at the table, long planks across sawhorses, spread with white tablecloths. The platters of ham and fried chicken were down to scraps, to wings and necks and backs; cakes were cut and crumbled; pieces of pie sat alone in their pans, waiting, Uncle Jess had said, for somebody fool enough to take the last one and have to kiss the cook; a little bit of everything was left—all kinds of salads, corn on the cob, peas, beans, sweet potatoes, okra.

"I'm gonna get me another piece of pink cake," Truett said, "if that old knothead ever gets through preaching."

"He's not preaching," the boy said. "He's speaking."

"You don't know anything," Truett said. "When you came to my house and spent the night, you washed your face with the rag my mother washes her bottom with."

"I didn't either. I didn't even wash my face."

The barn was dark and stifling. It smelled of mules and machinery, hay and dry corn and cows. Although the air did not stir, Cousin Orford's voice came through the big door as though on a sudden breeze: ". . . thicker—ah—than water. The sacred ties—ah—of friendship—ah—that is—ah—of family should never be broken—ah—asunder. . . ."

Truett was climbing up to the metal seat of some kind of machine. "Bet you don't even know what this is," he said.

The boy could see that you hitched mules to it, but what it did he had no idea. "You don't know either," he said.

Truett stopped, halfway into the seat, looking through the door. "Hey!"

The boy looked. "What?" he said. Cousin Orford was still speaking, everybody was still sitting there. Aunt Annie was fanning herself with a palmetto fan twice as big around as her head.

"Billy's waking up. He's gonna come looking for us." Truett scrambled down and ran to the other end of the the barn where a regular-sized door, cut into the large double doors, stood open enough to let a streak of sunlight in. It caught dust of straw down through the dark air. "Follow me," Truett said, squeezing past.

They ran down a slope beside a deep red gully and up into a thicket of pines. The boy looked back. "They can't see us from here," he said. He had on his fast tennis shoes, and he could have beat Truett there if he had known where they were going.

They lay down on the springy pine straw under the largest of the trees. Through the still needles the boy could see bright blue sky. One cloud was piled up white off to the side. At his home, in the evening about sunset, they would lie on the lawn and watch the high-piled clouds change from vanilla ice cream to banana to peach—his favorite—and sometimes to strawberry and raspberry. Jimmy, from down across the highway, would stand up and stick out his bare belly and rub it and say, "I scream, you scream, we all scream for ice cream," and flop back down on the grass.

"Gotta pee," Truett said. He went to the tree trunk and un-buttoned his pants. When he finished, he pointed to himself and said solemnly, "Girls bleed."

The boy thought a minute. "I bled last week," he said.

"Your peter?" Truett said.

"No. I had my tonsils out, and my throat started bleeding, and. . . ."

"That's not the same thing."

"And Mama called the doctor and he came to the house and pulled a big clot of blood out." His throat felt funny at the memory.

"Why didn't you swallow it?" Truett said. Suddenly he began running. "Beatcha to that big tree!" He was a long way ahead when the boy got on his feet, and the pine straw was too slippery to get a good start. But the boy knew he could run, loved to run. He sailed over the ground, side-stepping sticker bushes, leaping small gullies without effort. His feet did exactly what he wanted them to. Truett struggled to stay ahead, but the boy gained steadily. He was the best runner in his class. When Margaret Ann had made them all race around the schoolhouse to see which one she liked, he had left everybody behind.

The boy overtook Truett in a spurt and slapped the big pine tree as he went past it. "Beatcha!" he cried.

Truett stopped running. "No you didn't. I meant that sassafras, back yonder."

Through the Ages

Before the boy could answer, he heard a tiny voice shouting his name. He looked quickly for a place to hide, but his brother was already trotting toward them from the barn. If they ran away now, his mother would be angry.

Billy was yelling that something had happened; he was waving his hand wildly. The voice seemed thin and wordless as a bird's.

"We're not going to play with you," Truett shouted at him.

"What happened?" the boy was asking at the same time.

Truett's voice seemed to slow Billy's forward motion. He trudged the rest of the way with his lip stuck out. "You better," he said. "Mama said y'all better play with me."

"We'll play with you," the boy said. "What happened?"

"Jim got on that thing in the barn and it cut his hand and he's bleeding all over everything, and Granddaddy's doing something to it."

"Jim?" the boy said. Jim was his older brother. "Is it bad?"

"Real real bad," Billy said. "Let's play hide-and-seek. I'm not it."

"Well, I'm not it," Truett said.

The boy was running already. At first he could hear Truett grunting along behind and Billy yelling, "Wait for me!" Before long Billy was crying, screaming from the distance, "I'm gonna tell Mama on you!" He didn't care. He had to see if Jim was all right, and he wanted to run and run all by himself, away from Billy and Truett and everybody. The air on his cheeks was good. His feet in the tennis shoes flew. He had gone through the barn and up to the front steps of the house, had looked at the discolored bandage, at Jim's stiff face, at the awed cousins surrounding him, when Truett came up, red and sweating. "Is it bad?" the boy asked his brother.

Jim twisted his mouth. "Hit the bone."

"I bet it hurts."

Jim looked away. "Throbs," he said.

Billy came through the barn door, crying. Jim moved up the steps, and the boy started to come too. "I got to get a drink of water," Jim said. "Go play with Billy."

"I want to go with you," the boy said.

Jim shook his head impatiently. "Quit trying to tag along."

Jim had been hurt; nobody would tell him not to get water. The older cousins kept close to him, disappearing around the corner of the gallery. Truett stood on the steps beside the boy, panting. "I could go with them," he said, "if I wanted to."

"Well go ahead, and see if I care."

"I don't want to," Truett said. "I'm going to get another piece of that pink cake."

The boy knew that by now Billy had told his mother and that she would arrive at any moment. He did not turn to look. "Go on get your cake, then," he told Truett.

"Don't you want some?"

The boy shook his head; he actually didn't want any. All the cake in the world, right there waiting. He had looked forward to it, remembering the last reunion, hearing Jim talk about it. But after the chicken and everything, he had eaten only one piece of cake, the devil's food his mother had brought, and now he didn't want any at all.

"What do you mean?" his mother said, behind him. "Leaving this child out in that pasture all by himself! Running, just up from having your tonsils out, and already hemorrhaged once! I thought you had better sense."

"When are we going home?" the boy asked her.

His mother sighed. "It won't be long. Your Cousin Ed Williams is supposed to give a devotional before we leave. He's not as long-winded as Orford."

The three boys stood there until she had reached the shade, had joined the huddle of old people. Then Truett looked at Billy and said, "Tattletale."

"You better not hit me!"

"I'm gonna get you behind a bush and beat the snot out of you."

"You better not!"

The boy paid no attention to them, even though they followed as he walked slowly around the edge of the shade, the chairs, the old people. Some of the women were fanning the food to keep the flies off, and he heard one of them say, "She's three years and more older than *me*! *That's* how old she is!" He could hear the intermingled voices of aunts and uncles and cousins. An argument faded in for a moment as he passed, two men loud but without heat:

"No. First cousin once removed."

"I say second cousin."

"Not according to law."

"I'm not talking law. I'm talking kin."

It seemed to him that he was as old as any of them, that he had heard these same sounds at reunions all his life. He walked on, past all the shade, past the cars strung along a worn dirt trail at the front of the yard. He wanted to get away. He did not belong here, and there was the road. The August heat was nothing to him. He had only the faintest touch of sweat on his arms, although Truett's hair was plastered on his forehead and his face was still red.

"I'm going back to Grandmama's house," he said. There must have been rain within the past few days, because the road was packed and not all the red had faded out in the sun.

"That's three, four miles," Truett said.

"I don't care," the boy said. "I'm going to run it."

From out of the shade their grandmother came toward them, swishing her long skirt as though shooing chickens into a coop. "Come along! Make haste. Ed's fixing to give the devotional." She went back into the shade.

They didn't move. "I'm gonna tell," Billy said.

Truett scowled, but the boy caught his eye in warning. "Look," the boy said to Billy. "I'll bet you I can do it."

Truett nodded. "Yeah. Bet him, Billy. Bet him he can't."

Billy looked from one to the other. Then he grinned. "Betcha can't!"

"I'll be sitting in the swing when y'all drive up," the boy said. "But don't tell, or you'll lose the bet."

"Betcha can't!" Billy yelled.

"Shh!" Truett said. "Go on, if you're going," he told the boy. "Me and Billy'll get a piece of that cake."

The Hill

In the shade, heads were bowed. The boy walked to the road and only when he was shielded by the barn did he break into a run. He floated down a little slope and up the next rise, easy as a boat riding the waves. Free. He could see a buzzard gliding high over the pine tops. Off in a pasture cows were huddled like kinfolk beneath a cluster of trees.

Near the creek, trees moved in close to the road, the ground grew darker, the air felt damp. He loped evenly across the plank bridge. The water, tan as dust, flowed like a scar around an old snag. He thought suddenly that he tasted blood in his mouth. He was not supposed to exert himself, the doctor had said, but he had run fast in the pasture, had run up to see Jim's hand with no trouble. He did not break stride, but spit what little moisture was in his mouth out to the side. Clear. It was only the taste of blood, the ghost of blood. He rose out of the creek bottom, and that seemed for the moment what he was running to get away from.

There were a couple of forks to the road, and he had been unsure which to take. Each time he had turned without slowing toward whatever looked most familiar. And now, with his breath coming heavy, with the sweat pouring, he saw that he was right. Ahead was Scott Hill, the highest and steepest on the road. One winter, when it had rained for days, they had almost gone in the ditch here. The road had been nothing but red mud; the ditches were ragged and deep and they ran with heavy yellow water. The car had been sliding even where the road was flat, and his father said, "Well, here it comes," as they approached the hill. Halfway up it had washed out; one whole side was gone, a red gash, a hole. His sister, older than Jim even, had been frightened. His mother said nothing. Billy was lying in her lap, half asleep. Jim whistled a tune to keep up their courage.

His father got up speed, swishing the rear of the car like a fishtail, and they began to climb. The wheels spun; the car would slip to the side, catch, pull forward a few feet. It seemed that they would not get as far as the washout, but inch by inch they crawled alongside. The right rear tire was at the edge, slipping toward it. "Look out!" his sister cried, putting her hand over her eyes. Jim whistled louder. "Hang on," his father said, turning the wheel. The car seemed to be sliding sideways over the edge. Water full of earth poured down the ditch. The car caught, nudged forward, spun, sliding and spinning as though at the end of a rope. And then, miraculously, they crept upward, upward and over.

Today the hill was dry and whole. I can make it, the boy told himself. He tried to get the sweat out of his eyes with the back of his hand, but that only stung it in. He had been so caught up in the mud, the family, the car, that he was mounting the rise before he was ready. Jim's whistling echoed thinly in his ears; the taste of blood was still in his mouth; the uncertain footing of the car slurred his stride.

He could feel his heart pumping, feel his feet strike the unyielding ground. The road, blurred by sweat, joggled before him like a wall. He would not change stride, could not, he knew, without falling. Dry as his mouth was, the taste of blood was strong. Once he thought he felt a spurt from his throat, but when he tried he could spit nothing. His ears rang. He could hear the call of a redbird, or maybe a mockingbird. If he could hold the clear notes in his head, he told himself, he could make it.

He did not realize that he had reached the top of the hill until he felt himself going faster than his legs, pitching forward, swatting against the ground. He lay there until his eyes focused on a fence post, rotted out at the base, held up by strands of wire. Slowly, one motion at a time, he got up. He tried to wipe his eyes with his sleeve, but it was too short. He pulled out his shirttail, bent far over, pressed it to his eyes for a long time. Then he started walking; in a moment he was able to go into a trot. By the time the car pulled alongside he was running again.

The door opened beside him, and he stopped. His mother was leaning all the way across, holding the door handle. "Get in," she said. Her voice was shaking, the way his legs were. "Climb in here this instant!"

He stood still, trying to get it into his head. Air was rasping in and out of him. The car was within reach of his hand, the black surface with dust upon it, a thin cloud of dust settling all around.

"Are you trying to kill yourself?" Her voice broke. She came across the seat and over the running board, held him tightly against her. "Son," she said. "Son. You're all right aren't you? You're all right?"

Watering Place

The reunion was breaking up. Women were gathering their platters and bowls, men were stretching. He hung back as his mother went to get her dishes, but Truett rushed out of the shade to meet him. "How far'd you get?"

The boy shook his head. "Nearly there," he said finally. He walked through the gathering this time. As he passed, his Uncle Spurgeon was laughing, saying to somebody, "Old Ed really brought them violets up out of the '*de*-briss,' didn't he?"

Truett grabbed his arm. "Did you fall down?"

The boy nodded. He was out in the sunlight again, walking toward the house. The water was just around the corner of the gallery; he could feel it cold to his parched mouth already, washing down the taste of dust and of blood.

Billy was sitting on the bottom step, light hair, white skin you could almost see through. "Your mother told him he better not budge off that step," Truett said.

The boy stopped, waiting. Billy looked up at him defiantly. "I told Mama on you."

"I figured you did," the boy said.

"Truett wouldn't play with me anymore, and I told her."

"I ought to bloody your nose," the boy said. He could do it. Swat, just like that, and the skin would burst open. Cousin Orford had been saying something about Barnett blood by whatever name, shed for freedom.

"You better not!" Billy said, but the boy was already walking on.

"Here!" he heard his grandmother call. "Here! You boys get down off that gallery!"

But he did not look. He rounded the corner; the dipper, as he took it off the wall, rang like the whispered chime of a clock.

6 *Beyond the Garden*

In my mother's shoe box full of pictures there is one of me in the sweater with the argyle pattern that Uncle George bought because—who could believe it?—in New York it was chilly in August. The sweater long ago faded in the photograph toward the brown that it was, but so did the gray round stones beyond, the hills with vineyards and apple orchards in that utterly un-Mississippi country where the Catskills begin to rise.

New York; Sicilian relatives; 1936. It was not as if I had never traveled. For a week or two every summer I had gone with my father to a revival meeting, to Carthage or Lena or Hickory. When I was four he took me all the way to Calhoun, Georgia, on a train that went through a tunnel near Chattanooga. We slept together in a rocking Pullman berth, his hand holding my hand holding his thumb. In a bright yard the pastor's wife showed me how to make yellow and pink snapdragons snap.

As a family we had often driven the fifty or so miles from our house on Clinton Boulevard to my grandmother's in Standing Pine, and the summer just past we had ventured all the way to the Gulf coast in our Model A, delayed, as I remember it, by only one flat tire. Our friends there took us in rowboats out to Deer Island's long strip of sand for a weenie roast. As dark came on, we could see another bonfire down the island toward the brush and trees; later, when it had died to a distant touch of light, we heard a clear voice singing "Smoke Gets in Your Eyes." A local girl, they said, home from New York where she was in opera. When we rowed back to the mainland in the dark, each stroke of the oars stirred a pale green phosphorescence.

Our Sicilian relatives were not completely unknown to us either. From their farm near Amite, Louisiana, Aunt Fanny (zia Ninfa, she would have been if we had known the language) and Uncle Dominic Lupo shipped us a crate of strawberries every year; we'd eat them on cereal and on shortcake, crank them into homemade ice cream, cook them down with sugar into preserves to be eaten with hot biscuits and butter. Long afterward the frail baskets would be used around the house, thin wood faintly blotched with red; hold one to your nose and be tantalized by ghosts of strawberries, an unknown state, kinfolk you had never seen.

Once we drove down to visit them and their ten children. I had not imagined that the field the strawberries came from would be so flat, the plants so low to the ground. Between the strawberry field and the house there was a huge brick oven; the loaves Aunt Fanny took out of it in great batches had a thick, tough crust. I sat on the steps, looking toward the mulberry tree, a chunk of fresh bread in one hand, a chunk of homemade white cheese in the other. A bite of cheese, a bite of bread, and my Sicilian blood distilled into my brain the essence of a word I had never heard: Squisite! Why I have never found bread and cheese like that again—in New York, California, Sicily—I don't know. Perhaps Aunt Fanny cooked the way my grandmother in Standing Pine did: a pinch of this, a handful of that, and, "I declare, Mabel, I don't know why it came out different. I made it just like I did the last time."

Aunt Fanny was short, heavy, dark. Uncle Dominic I remember as thinner, relatively tall; he had not taken to English as well as she, called the stickers we hurt our bare feet on "grass wit da pain." The children must have ranged from my age upward. I remember mostly three or four of them: the girl who saw to us, and boys with mischievous brown eyes who would bring us from the tree dark shiny mulberries. No matter how gently you held them, they left your palm sweet with purple stains.

If I saw any of the rest of my father's family before 1936, I don't remember it, but they, too, sent gifts. From the two sets of Canzoneris and the Masaracchias, we would get Christmas boxes of crescent-shaped anise cookies with hard white icing and little candy sprinkles; long rolled fig cakes, broken into chunks; and pignulate: hard pastry balls molded together with honey into sticky pine cones—food like nothing we knew of in Mississippi, from family that had to be different from any we knew, distant and foreign as they were. We could not imagine them, except for Tony, who was known, it seemed, to everybody. "Are you any kin . . . ?" store clerks would ask, and we would answer modestly, "First cousin," heart giving a little flip. How did we manage to be first cousins to the lightweight champion of the world, a real Italian, a New Yorker we knew only through pictures, newspapers, radio?

My father's brothers and sisters had married Sicilians; they kept their ties with the language, the customs, other Sicilians. We had only the difficult last name, my father's accent, his occasional stories about the Old Country, and a couple of Sicilian phrases: Mangia pane, and Chiuia porta—a mere whiff of garlic in the land of fried chicken and string beans. The anticipation of seeing so many unknown foreign relatives at once, when Uncle George sent for us in 1936, would have stirred in us enough excitement for several normal years. But there was also the fact that it was New York we were going to, making me the most cosmopolitan member of the sixth grade—which I would enter dramatically, on our return, a week late—surpassing even my friend who had been all the way to Colorado. And we would actually meet Tony, so that when we had modestly answered, "First cousin," and then the clerk said, "No kidding? Do you know him?" we could modestly respond, "Sure." It had even been arranged, as though for our benefit, that he would defend his title while we were there.

The brand new wood-paneled Ford station wagon Uncle George was sending down would all by itself have been glory enough for my brothers and me in those meager days. There was no way to know, of course, that this would be the only time my father's family in this country would all be together—Aunt Fanny and her family had moved to a farm near Uncle George's—or that the gathering was to occur precisely halfway between my father's departure from Sicily, in 1903, and his only visit back, in 1969.

One of Aunt Josephine's younger brothers, Tony Schiro, drove the station wagon down to Louisiana, to leave his wife and child with her family, and came back for us late on the appointed day. Time after time over the years, isolated as we were out from town, we stood at the front windows or in the front yard, as we did that August evening, and watched every car coming up the highway from the west, every set of lights, until it seemed that whoever it was would never come. And then the shout, "That's him! That's him!" A flurry, and, miraculously, we were crammed into our seats, relishing the new car smell. We rolled down the driveway to Highway 80, turned right, and—did we say, as we sometimes did, Good-bye house, good-bye trees? Or did we hold that inside because of the stranger driving us away?

It is hard to imagine now the seven of us in that 1936 Ford marveling at the luxury and space. Tony Schiro; Dad; Mom; Antonina, full-grown at sixteen; Joe Boy, a six-foot fourteen-year-old; me at ten; George Arden, eight. And we plotted our trip the long way round, to miss most of the mountains as well as the area where polio was epidemic.

Late that night we stopped at a tourist home in Selma, Alabama, got up early and made it through Atlanta and into the Blue Ridge Mountains by dark. My father swapped off with Tony Schiro, and they decided to drive through the night. On what must have been a detour, in a pouring rain, Dad slushed and skidded us around a muddy mountain road that dropped off on our left into blackness, headlights swinging from blank rain to sheer rock and back again.

Trapped, my mother and father had to watch Tony take an occasional swig from the half pint he kept in the glove compartment, to keep himself alert. I had never seen anyone drink anything stronger than coffee. "He seems to know what he's doing," my mother said hopefully. "He's a very good driver."

We drove up through New Jersey, down through the roaring Holland Tunnel with the entire Hudson River over our heads, and stopped in traffic right beside the tallest building in the world. We stuck our heads out the back window and strained to look upward. A cab driver in the next lane gave us an Empire State Building lecture, how many stories, how many feet to the top. Back over the Hudson on the George Washington Bridge, up through Newburgh, out to Marlboro. On the right of the narrow road, a big swimming pool in front of a low building, then the large white summer hotel, the square stucco training building, the horse barns off beyond. Rocky hills, vineyards, orchards. Close in on the left, a white-trunked weeping birch, a big two-story white house. Relatives. In some large room they passed us down a line, hugging, kissing, crying. I could see my younger brother ahead of me, drawn back stiffly as if in terror as they grabbed him one from another.

Tony's wife, Rita, said later that I was the only one who kissed her back. I squirmed; I hadn't kissed her; I'd certainly have remembered it if I had dared. She was a showgirl, so dark and beautiful, so sleek and bold, so touched with lipstick and mascara that it would have been a sin to look directly at her if she weren't married to your cousin.

For two weeks we lived a strange and fascinating life in a strange and fascinating world. The day no longer began when the grass was wet with dew (back home my grandmother and Old Bob, the black man who lived near us, were milking the cows and feeding the chickens while we were gone); it started about noon, with lunch, when we would ordinarily have been eating our dinner of vegetables from the garden. The serious eating began about our bedtime. In the hotel dining room Uncle George would preside over a long table seating perhaps twenty people: our family, his family, some kinfolks staying at the hotel (I remember a three-year-old whose mouth came just to the edge of his plate, scooping in spaghetti with a tablespoon and crying because it wouldn't go in his mouth sideways), and three or four dark-suited men who were there for the upcoming fight. I didn't know enough then to speculate on their connections, and I don't know enough now to do more than wonder.

The waiters would serve platters of antipasto, then spaghetti—with a different sauce every night and every one delicious. One sauce, the flavor of which still lingers enough to set my mouth watering, must have been made from something like the fresh pink anchovies that the Osteria of Fresh Fish in Palermo lays out across their green salads. We would gorge ourselves on the spaghetti—a whole meal when we had it at home, and enough for a meal here—then sit stuffed and dismayed as they brought in the main course. Steaks I remember. And once snails, imported from Italy. I pried one from its shell, chewed as little as possible, and managed to keep it down. Fruit, nuts, cheese, wine. Uncle George would raise his glass, the others would raise theirs: "Salute."

Sometimes in the afternoon we would sit in the lobby and

listen to the jukebox playing "Empty Saddles in the Old Corral," or "It's a Sin to Tell a Lie," or

> All the jive is gone,
> All the jive is gone,
> So come on in and drink some gin
> Cause all the jive is gone.

A tall fair young man with a mop of blond hair (we called him Bushy) would ask my sister to dance, and she'd shake her head. He did not understand us. We didn't dance, bet, play cards with poker decks, or—worst of all—drink. The bar just off the lobby was a dark cave from which came voices, the clink of glasses, the spreading, heady odor of liquor.

No one used the swimming pool while we were there. It was in the days when a choking yellow liquid was sprayed up our noses to ward off polio, and swimming was forbidden. But we could visit the barns and see huge draft horses for the first time—elephants and locomotives of horses. And we could ride the saddle horses. My younger brother and I were restricted to a docile old mare, not allowed on the young horse that was much faster, but had, unfortunately, a real love for the stable. Once my older brother was headed out at a brisk gallop when the horse swapped ends; suddenly it was coming back at the same pace and my brother was running in the direction they had been going. After that I no longer begged to ride the fast horse.

We walked up the hills into the orchards, played in the vineyards around Aunt Fanny's house, took her kids "snipe hunting" among the grapevines. We went to Aunt Vincent's apartment in Newburgh, to Uncle Cyrus's butcher shop where we watched him make up sausage in two huge batches, one for Americans, the other—he covered it with red pepper and kneaded it in—for Italians. We ventured a taste of the hot sausage that night at his house. He looked so much like my father of a few years before that we told each other he looked more like Dad than Dad did.

One day we drove up to the Schiro farm, in sight of the gray Catskills. The low farmhouse and barn, with their thick, hand-hewn beams, were twice as old as anything we knew, the Old Capitol in Jackson, even, or what everybody called the Historic Old Chapel in Clinton, both of which had survived the Civil War. Somebody took us to a Revolutionary War fort high above the Hudson. Far off across the river, the longest train we'd ever seen crawled along like a thin black worm.

Aunt Josephine seemed to live in the kitchen. I watched her making cheese in huge steaming pots. When the curds would gather, a couple of men (there seemed to be an endless supply of young men, all relatives) would pour it off into woven baskets, press it, dump the formed hoops into barrels of brine in the cool cellar, which was musty with the odor of the curing cheese and of wine in huge barrels. Once when the curds were ready the young men were not at hand, and Aunt Josephine asked me to run tell Joe, her oldest son, to come help. I found him standing with Uncle George in the living room, arguing in Sicilian. I stood timidly under the two heavy men and waited. Finally there was a pause, and I plunged in: "Aunt Josephine wants you to come help in the kitchen." Joe looked down at me, his mind still obviously on the discussion. "Go get somebody else," he said impatiently. "Can't you see we're talking business?" I was crushed, mortified. Many years later I saw him again, a small, genial, white-haired man who had been suffering heart attacks. He was tending bar at a bowling alley where he was so well liked that business had tripled since he started working there. It was as if the thirty-five years between were a split second: one instant I was ten years old, looking up at a threatening thundercloud, and, flash, I was forty-five, looking down at the untroubled surface of a pool. I felt as though he had reversed directions, like the stable-loving horse, and left me stumbling on ahead to keep my balance.

I do not know how the memory chooses what things to hold intact. The taste of fresh ricotta with a mild cherry jelly and flaky biscuits. Some kid chanting, "If you don't vote for Landon, you'll land on the streets." The knock-knock names that seemed daring to me: Helen the basement, and Philip a mug with beer. People laughing at us for saying "Over yonder." The unused Dusenberg limousine we'd sit in and pretend to drive—somebody ruined in the '29 crash had passed it on to Uncle George in lieu of money owed. Old Mr. Izzy, his belly shoved far out over his belt, his puffy face puffing on a dead cigar, rounding up the whole flock of kids for a treat when the ice cream truck tinkled into hearing.

Lavish old Mr. Izzy. I associated him with Tony's account of Dinty Moore in his New York restaurant. Dinty Moore would come to your table, greet you, Tony said, and ask what you had ordered. You'd say, "A hamburger." Dinty Moore would gesture grandly to the waiter. "Bring 'im a *big* hamburger." You'd get the regular size. If you wanted change for a dime to play the jukebox, Dinty Moore would say, "Give him a *handful* of nickels." You'd get two nickels. Mr. Izzy not only made the grand gesture, he actually handed out handfuls of nickels, to the ice cream man every morning, with a flourish. He had been something—a trainer, I think—in Tony's camp years before. Now he was an ex-trainer in Tony's camp.

We were sitting in the house one afternoon when Tony and Rita came over from the hotel lobby. As soon as they got in the door Rita said, "Now will you tell me why you kept reading the newspaper aloud?" She turned to us. "He'd say, 'Hey, Rita, did you see this about Roosevelt on the front page?' And I'd say, 'Yeah, I saw it.' And then he'd read it to me anyway."

Tony laughed. "I couldn't say anything there. It was for Izzy."

"For Izzy? He was sitting off in the corner cleaning his fingernails. He wasn't paying attention to you."

"He was memorizing everything I read. He's over there right now telling Nick or somebody, 'Hey, did you see that about Roosevelt on the front page today?'"

Rita looked at him for a moment. They were newly married. "Oh," she said finally.

"I've done it for years," Tony said. "You'll get used to it."

We got to watch Tony training for the fight. He would jump rope so fast the rope was a blur, switching hands, crossing his feet, talking and laughing all the while with the people sitting in folding chairs a safe distance back from the ring. He was trim, fast, good-natured; he had a wide spontaneous smile. One of his sparring partners was a redhead who'd begin to flush after a few minutes of being tapped in the face by Tony's gloves; suddenly he'd quit sparring and start to move in for the kill, only to land on his back in the same instant. We believed that we couldn't even see Tony's hands move from where they were cocked low at his sides.

The day of the fight the place emptied, leaving my mother, my sister, my younger brother, and me there at the house with Aunt Josephine, who could not stand to watch her son in the ring. My older brother was big enough and lucky enough to pass for eighteen. I'd have given anything to go with the men to Madison Square Garden and watch Tony beat his old sparring partner, Lou Ambers, who had the audacity to challenge him. I tried to sit a little apart from the women and my kid brother when the fight came on the radio.

It soon became apparent that the announcer was against Tony; he kept saying that Tony was tiring, that he couldn't keep his guard up, when everybody knew that was his fighting style. But we began really to worry when he described the cut near Tony's eye, the blood pouring down his face. Aunt Josephine kept her hand to her face, giving little cries of pain. She seemed to care only that the fight was over, finally, not that Ambers was announced the winner and new champion.

Tony really didn't lose, the men assured us when they returned. He didn't look as though he had lost. The small cut on his face had no relationship to its bloody description on the radio. He was in good spirits, laughing and joking. The men told us that Tony had in fact won so decisively that Ambers tried to leave the ring, was halfway through the ropes, headed for the dressing room, when referee Arthur Donovan pulled him back and, to his obvious amazement, held up his hand.

Except occasionally on television, when he would be introduced in the ring before a Friday night fight, I saw Tony only once again. He had tried a comeback that ended when, according to an Associated Press sports page obituary I still have, he was knocked out on November 1, 1939, by Al "Bummy" Davis. Later Tony became a nightclub comic, doing imitations of Jimmy Durante, and was associated with "a Broadway restaurant which bore his name," to quote from the same obituary. He and Rita had a daughter. Some time before I took my father to see him in 1959—I don't know just when—they were divorced.

He had come down to Shreveport to be installed in the Ark-La-Tex Sports Hall of Fame—claimed by Louisiana because he had been born in Independence and had begun fighting in New Orleans. He still had the wide smile, and although he was overweight, he still moved so lightly that it seemed his feet didn't quite touch the floor. A couple of men swept into the country club with him for the awards dinner, handling everything, arranging for him. One of them grabbed my hand and said, "I'm So-and-so, from one of the richest families in New Orleans." In the few minutes they allowed us with him, Tony said, "Yes, Rita's married again and lives in Hollywood. She's happy, and so I'm happy." The smile didn't hold. The eyes shifted aside. When it came his turn to accept his award, he told the joke about the man carrying a grandfather clock to the shop and the drunk asking if he couldn't afford a watch.

Later that year Tony's body was found a couple of days after he had dropped dead in his hotel room in New York. They were going to have a large police escort for the funeral procession, his brother told me a dozen years afterward, but new city rules prevented it. His sister added that he was handled by the same undertaker who later handled Judy Garland.

Back then, in 1936, the loss to Ambers seemed no big thing. Tony was in good shape. He seemed confident. After all, this was the fifth championship he'd won and had either abandoned or lost. We weren't worried. It was my defeat, anyway, only as it reflected upon me; I had my own defeats to brood upon. I could see myself now as an ineffective errand boy, a kid too little for the fast horse, not big enough to go to the fight, so constrained he had to change the knock-knock punch line to Philip a glass with milk. Too shy to have really kissed Rita back.

The laughter of the waiters still rang in my ears from the time my cousin Lilly sent me to the hotel kitchen to get her dog some scraps. Nick Schiro and the others gathered around while I told what I wanted. They directed my request to the chef, who went into a long, incomprehensible speech. I waited politely until he had finished. "I'm sorry," I told him, "but I don't speak Italian." Nick put his hand on my shoulder. "He was speaking English," he said. Why did I see myself as from the back, standing before the gesticulating chef who stood before a background of huge pots? Would a slight move of the head have brought into perspective the fact that nobody but me saw what I saw, to nobody but me it was real?

It would be thirty-five years before I'd find out that our visit made so little impression on our cousins that some of them had no memory of it at all, not even Tony's youngest brother, about eighteen at the time, who stuffed himself into the station wagon with us and made the whole long trip southward. I remember his shouting, "Hi, good-looking," out the window at a pretty girl crossing at a traffic light in South Carolina. She stopped, looked at him steadily, said, "Hello, handsome," and walked on before he could recover. I was squeezed into the back seat, silent, admiring, and apparently invisible.

Before that we had stopped for some sightseeing. In the

top of the Washington Monument, captivated by the city spread out below and by the mere fact of height, I turned impulsively to someone I thought was my mother, tugged on her hand, begged, "Let's walk down, Mom, please," looked up into the eyes of a woman startled for that single instant of her life into looking down at me.

The state of Virginia was trying to protect her apple trees that year; we were stopped at the border while officials looked through the luggage for fresh fruit. My father stood by, prancing with apprehension. What if they found the two bottles of wine his older brother had made him take home—him, Brother Joe, a worker for the Lord? My mother laughed at him as we drove on. "They didn't know you from Adam, anyway," she told him, but it did not ease his mind. He had done everything he could to keep from taking the wine, but Uncle George had prevailed. "I may come see you someday," he had said finally, "and you can serve it to me." When we got home, my father poured out the wine and buried the bottles far out back, beyond the garden.

7 *Revival*

I used to hold my mother's hand mirror flat under my nose so that the hanging light fixture rose like a glass flower up to my waist; then I would turn with great care, step over the top of the door into the hall, and walk through the house on the quaking plaster of the ceiling. Or I would face the hand mirror to the larger mirror over the dresser and watch precise frames swing into an infinite corridor of empty doorways.

What flat silvered glass could do to a familiar scene fascinated me. A rectangle of sunlight across the quilt on my parents' bed would be the brightest spot in the reflected room. The colored patches looked richer in the mirror, perhaps, but in that world of mere light nothing could release the warm smell of cotton cut and sewn by my grandmother's hand. Move your head and perspective would strike you like a catch of the breath: the chair would slide across a couple of inches of bed; the bedpost edge over to show the corner of the door frame; the door frame shy aside just enough to reveal a tall sliver of dining room, seen clearly through the dark hall.

When nobody else was around, how could I resist trying to find out what I looked like? Except the mirrors turned me left-handed, shifted the mole to the other cheek. Abraham Lincoln had a mole there, but the face with it was craggy. The way my hair fell across one eye, I could hold the end of a comb under my nose and look more like Adolph Hitler. The only thing I could really watch myself do, anyway, was watch myself. The face around those eyes that I could never catch off guard is, at least by now, a blur.

What image I have of the boy I was is recalled from snapshots: big eyes, wide ears under the turned-up flaps of an aviator cap, skinny legs sticking out of short pants, mouth quirked as though trying not to break into a laugh—he is one of six or eight kids standing in the yard at home, with the edge of the gravel driveway at their sneakered toes, the front porch behind them.

The Word

Sometimes the boy would sit with his father behind the unfolded morning paper and read the funnies, except he would be through and waiting by the time his father's eyes moved from Dick Tracy down to Little Orphan Annie. If his mother passed by on her way from making up the beds to cleaning up the breakfast dishes, she'd stop in the wide doorway to the dining room and look at them there on the wicker davenport. "I declare, Joe; you can waste half a day reading the comic strips." His father would not hear her. "Waste," she'd say. "Total and absolute waste. What could you possibly get out of those things? You'd think you were studying the Scriptures." His father did study the Bible the same way, only with his finger moving from word to word. "Well, they're not the Scriptures," she'd say, "and they're not the garden that ought to be hoed before the heat of the day." His father would be reading Sandy's balloon, saying it slowly to himself as though letting all its significance sink in: "Arf."

"Joe!" His mother's voice would come so sudden and loud that he would jump. "Joe Canzoneri!"

His father's eyes would pull slowly from the page the way

you stretch bubble gum out with your fingers. "Had what?" It was what he always said when he realized somebody was talking to him.

"You haven't heard a word I've said. You'd do better to hoe those beans before it's too hot to breathe."

His father's eyes would still not have lost their absorption in Little Orphan Annie. "Bob and I just read the funny paper."

His mother had a way of setting her jaw. "Just read the funny paper," she'd say, mocking his father. "Then it'll be the crossword puzzle till I've got dinner on the table." And this time she went on to say, "You have to write that letter to Richmond, too, if you're going to do it. You can drag that out for the rest of the day."

"Oh," his father said. "Yeah," eyes pulling back to the paper. "I better do that."

She stood there a minute longer. Finally she just shook her head. "If you're right, the Lord sure enough does work in mysterious ways. And he'd better perform some of his wonders pretty soon."

He knew what his mother was talking about. They needed money to make the payment on the house, to buy cowfeed, cornmeal, sugar. His father had been in a revival meeting up in the delta, but he'd led the singing, not preached, and they split the offering so the preacher got sixty percent and he got forty. He'd come home Sunday for a week off, which meant no money. Every morning except this one he had worked in the garden till his overalls were soaked and dripping, and then he'd rest flat on his back on the kitchen floor. He was lying there Monday so quietly that he heard the mailman all the way from the highway. "I get it," he said, hurrying to his feet. He came back up the driveway with a handful of letters. "If only I'd beat you to the mailbox that one time," his mother had said over and over since. The first letter his father opened was an invitation to preach and sing for two weeks at Wanilla, a little church in the country out from Brookhaven.

The next was an invitation for the same two weeks at the First Baptist Church of Richmond, Virginia. The rest were bills.

His mother had sat down at the kitchen table and sighed. "Richmond. Thank the Lord. That'll just about get us through the summer."

His father had stood there, still dripping wet. "I go to Wanilla," he said.

"Wanilla. Have you lost your mind?"

He sat down, too, and picked up the letters, one and then the other. "The Lord lead me to open this letter first."

"The Lord didn't stack the mail. Mr. Rochester did that."

He shook his head slowly and said nothing.

"If the Lord hadn't wanted you to go to Richmond, why did he lead them to invite you?" She put her head in her hands. "You're not the only one the Lord deals with. What if he leads me to say take Richmond and cash money instead of a handful of change and a couple of gallons of molasses? "

"I have to do what God say."

"The only reason you're free to 'do what God say' is that I keep up your house and garden and four children, not to mention two cows and a yardful of chickens and that useless dog. But that doesn't count for anything."

He spread his hands. "The Lord take care of us, Mabel."

"He takes care of you, all right. But why does it always have to be through the sweat of my brow?"

Half the afternoon his father sat in front of the portable Royal at the dining room table. Now and then he'd stiffen one finger on each hand and poke three or four keys in succession. Then he'd peer at what he'd written, sit a while longer, strike again. The typewriter keys were round, the kind with rims holding circles of glass over the letters. If you stood near the china cabinet, the light through the side door blanked them out.

He stood there till his father pulled the paper out, read the couple of lines with long deliberation, signed his name. Then he moved to his father's side. "I'll go to Lena, I guess."

His father put his arm around him. "Good. We have a good time." He folded the letter carefully and ran a blunt thumbnail down the crease. He rolled a small envelope into the typewriter, moved the carriage back and forth slowly, checking to see that it was straight. "I don't use typewriter like you sister," his father said. She took typing in school; her fingers hovered over the keyboard, rattling out the letters like hail. "Somebody say I use method he call . . . H. F. C.? Something like that."

"H. P. C.," he told his father.

"Yeah." His father laughed. "Stand for Hunt, and . . . something he say. . . ."

"Hunt, Peck, and Cuss."

His father laughed again. "Hunt, Peck, and Cuss, somebody say. I do that, sure 'nough, only the Lord help me not cuss." He shook his head. "I declare, if the Lord didn't give me sense of humor, see the funny side of thing, I don't know what I do."

"You want to go Lena with me next week," his father had asked him at dinner, "or wait and go to Wanilla?"

"I'm going where they've got a pickle factory," his younger brother said.

"You went there last year," his older brother said. They had all driven down to get his father and younger brother and got to go through the pickle factory too. It was just an old tin-roofed shed; they climbed up onto the high wooden walkways between huge vats of brine. "Don't fall in," his younger brother told him; you'd think he owned the pickle factory.

"I'm going again." His younger brother poked out his bare stomach and rubbed it. "I'm going to eat a hundred pickles."

"And die with a bellyache," his older brother said.

"Don't say that," his mother said.

"Why not? That would give anybody a bellyache."

"Say stomachache."

"If I said stomachache, they'd laugh me off the school bus."

His sister got up from the table. "They'd do that just from looking at you."

"Well, you don't have to worry. Nobody'd look at that face of yours."

"Where are you going?" his mother asked his sister. "You haven't eaten enough to keep a bird alive."

"Make him leave me alone. He makes me sick."

"You started it," his brother said. "So quit your bellyaching."

"Be ashamed, both of you," his mother said. She turned to his father. "Can't you tend to your children just once?"

His father looked up, a forkful of peas halfway to his mouth. "Had what?"

The Tree

After dinner, when his father took the typewriter from its case, the boy went outside to think. The sun was very hot on his bare shoulders, and the ground was so packed and dry where he went through the pasture fence that it burned his feet. He hurried toward the clump of oaks; the cows were standing in the shade, tails switching. He stopped to pat old Blackface, and she swung her head aside to nuzzle him. Fenwick tossed her horns; she was younger, and sometimes on cool days she would run and buck just for the fun of it. In the winter he enjoyed milking old Blackface while his older brother milked Fenwick across the stall. He would put his head against the warm flank, smell the warm milk, listen as his brother sang hillbilly songs through his nose or preached crazy sermons in a voice like a radio preacher, making them up as he went. Sometimes Kaiser would bark at the stall door, and his brother would squirt milk through the crack and tickle his nose.

The tallest of the half dozen oaks was his tree. He took hold of the bottom limb he used to have to jump for, walked up the trunk until he could swing a leg over, and climbed slowly to the top. The next tree, nearly as tall as his, was his younger brother's. Sometimes they pretended they were in the crow's nests of old sailing ships, shouting to each other over a heavy sea. Sometimes they just talked. This was the only place they really talked to each other, high in their separate trees, across the empty space where the limbs didn't quite touch.

He had been to Wanilla with his father before. You went on the G. M. & N. railroad, on the one-car Doodlebug that was kind of like the Toonerville Trolley; the streamlined Rebel didn't stop there. The town was only the depot, a store, a couple of houses, and the white church in sight down the road. Maybe you could count the nearest farm, where a boy about his age lived; he bragged that his birthday was January 19, the same as Robert E. Lee. He had gone swimming with that boy's family in the creek behind the church, where they baptized people, and then he had walked by himself all the way out to the Edwards' farm, where he and his father were staying. But his father wasn't there; he had gone, Mrs. Edwards told him, to the house near the depot, for supper. He trudged the dusty road back. When he got there they were already eating. "I thought they bring you here," his father said. The boy sat down, took one bite, and without knowing he would do it, started to cry. "He's just exhausted," his father said. It was the first time he'd ever heard the word.

A slight breeze swayed the tree, and he held tightly to the trunk. He could feel the rough bark printing itself into his side.

He did not want to go to Wanilla, to the dim church with the slatted pews where his father once preached so late that the Rebel came through before he finished, long blasts of the whistle shattering toward them and rushing away in the night. But he did not want to go to Lena, either, to unknown people and a strange house to sleep in. It was the only time he hadn't wanted to go with his father since he first went to Utica when he was three years old. They'd held him up to pull the bell rope hanging through a little round hole in the ceiling, and he would cry when his father got up to lead the singing.

There was always something he did wrong. Up at Catchings, his father had to get after him for giggling in church every time the boy in front threw his thumb out of joint. At Carthage, he got sick and had to be driven home. At Hickory, he couldn't bring himself to ask the people where the bathroom was and wet his pants.

His father wanted him to go again this year, anyway, and he could imagine how hurt his father would look if he said no. He might as well go on to Lena and get it over with. You went there on the G. M. & N. too, he knew, only you went north instead of south. The phrase struck him: north instead of south. He looked at the house, the gray roof shingles, the brick chimneys, the front porch facing the same way he was facing, toward the highway. In his mind Wanilla had been in front of him, but that was north, and Wanilla was south. He closed his eyes and hugged the tree trunk. You'd think anybody would know the directions where he had lived ever since he could remember, but he kept getting them backward, as if somebody had stuck a pin right where the house was and had turned the map around it so that all the words were upside down. He had to force the world back around in his head until what the house faced was north, until Wanilla was behind him and Lena swung into place ahead—northeast, really—off to the right a little, out of sight beyond the highway, the trees.

It made him dizzy, the way he had felt the night he'd looked out the car window and realized that there must be something past the stars, and something past whatever was past the stars, and something past that, and on and on forever. The same dizziness he felt every time his thoughts got too near the dark emptiness inside that was like a black hole in his mind.

Chorus

The sun slanted in the open window, lighting the pews on the other side of the church. It was not hot yet; morning services would start in half an hour, when the pastor led the visiting preacher in and they sat solemnly in the high-backed chairs. Now his father was standing in front of a handful of kids; a woman in a thin flowered dress waited at the piano.

"I love children," his father said. "You see, Jesus say, 'Suffer the little children to come unto me. . . .' "

He looked away. You don't say, "I love children" to a bunch of kids, he wanted to tell his father. But he knew it didn't matter; people liked his father so much they didn't care when he said things like that.

"I may not sing ver' good," his father was saying with a little laugh, "and maybe I say words funny, but I try do what the Lord say and make a joyful noise."

The preacher who was here for the revival seemed more like what a preacher was supposed to be. "Just call me David," he'd said when they met; "I'm a preacher's kid too." Some of the older men said he had great promise, the Lord would use him in a big way, as he had David in the Bible. He was just out of college, slender, tall, slightly pale. He wore a white suit and white shoes, and out of doors a straw hat; from under the stiff brim his blue eyes looked upon the world as if in judgment.

"Listen," his father was saying. His face clouded. His face and his voice changed, his hands, shoulders, body moved with everything he said. " 'Let no man despise thy youth.' Paul say that to Timothy, but God mean it for you too."

He focused on the hymnal in the rack before him. In a while his father would get around to the singing, to the choruses he taught all his junior choirs. The first one would be "In the Sweet Bye and Bye," and when he got to the line

Won't it be glorious when I get there,

his father would say it like a cross between won't and wouldn't:

Wunt it be glorious when I get there;

and all the kids, hanging onto every word, every note, would
sing it the same way:

Wunt it be glorious when I get there!

The boy loved maps, had loved them since Mrs. Lassetter
taught them geography in the fourth grade and they had had
contests, trying to be the first to point to whatever city or state
or river she called out. He always thought of the United States
as it was on the map that pulled down in front of the
blackboard, right where during recess one day somebody had
drawn a circle and beside it what looked so much like a
banana that it took him a minute to understand why some of
the kids snickered and the teacher was upset. Now on that
map in his mind he could mark off the whole Southland his
father had traveled, a vast slab of land from New Mexico
nearly to Maryland, from above the Ohio River all the way
down to Florida, the Gulf, the Rio Grande; he could remember the colors of the various states, imagine the line of
mountains where Kentucky and Virginia, Tennessee
nd North Carolina came together, the hills of pines and oaks
through Alabama and over to the flat black Mississippi delta
shoulder-high with cotton, and on across to the dry open
plains of Texas spreading westward to the Rockies. He could
see sprinkled over this expanse the dots, the tiny circles, the
stars that stood for towns and cities and state capitals, each
with at least one Baptist church his father had been to—white
plank churches among scrub oaks; low brick churches with
painted palm trees and a blue River Jordan snaking down
into the baptistry; massive stone churches with huge windows
of stained glass, with cushioned pews and aisles thickly car-
peted. Hundreds of churches holding thousands of children,
faces scrubbed and eyes alight, all singing,

I'll have a mansion so bright and so fair,
Wunt it be glorious when I get there!

The Ministry

"He's ver' young," his father was saying, "but the Lord use him. He learn. Gotta few craz' notion from some postmillennialist book, but I try show him what God say."

Mr. Davis nodded. He never said much. They were in the Davises' breakfast nook, drinking coffee as they did every night after services.

"And I try say a few things to the people, in song service, not be confused what God say. And when I tol' my experience tonight."

The boy's eyes were tired and hot. As long as his milk had kept the glass cold, he would hold it tight and then put his hand over his eyes, but now he had drunk all the milk. "I think I'll go on to bed," he told his father.

"You go by you'self?" His father opened his arms; he got up and hugged him goodnight, kissed the whiskery cheek. "Goodnight, Kerflumox. I be there in a minute."

"Night," he said. "Night, Mr. Davis." He did not look at Mr. Davis. Why did his father have to call him Kerflumox in front of somebody? He went through the dining room with the fine china and silver shining from the polished cabinet, into the living room with its heavy drapes and soft carpet, up the silent stairs past the closed door where Mrs. Davis was already asleep, probably.

The light in the bedroom was on. If it hadn't been, he'd have reached around the door frame to find the switch, risking only his hand and arm. At home he would force himself to go into the bedroom before turning on the light; sometimes if his hand didn't touch the switch first thing, he would jump back through the door in spite of himself. Once, without even trying to turn on the light, he had made it almost to the middle of the room before he couldn't stand it, and then he held himself almost to a walk going back to the hall.

The pillow felt cool to his face, but too soft and smooth, too full. It was Thursday, a whole week after he had decided to come, and he had to spend tonight and tomorrow night here, and then they'd take the Rebel back to Jackson. His mother would meet them at the station near the Old Capitol, and they'd drive all the way out Capitol Street past the zoo and cross over the bridge beside the woods where he could feel by the cool air he was getting toward home.

Kaiser would jump up on him and bark, waggle around so that he could scratch his ears and just above his cutoff tail at the same time. He missed Kaiser more than anything. He had spent the whole afternoon out in the country with Herbert, shooting his Benjamin air rifle that you could pump so hard the BBs would bury themselves in a fence post, but even then he'd rather have been playing with Kaiser, chasing each other around the yard and tumbling together. When the sun went down, he'd go to the little coop for baby chickens and Kaiser would jump up on it and sit there beside him watching the colors spread over the whole western sky, with the one tall hickory tree down beyond the sloping pasture like a finger touching the edge to see if the paint was wet. Kaiser would turn to lick his ear and then look back at the sunset.

He had to quit thinking about that. He ached all down through his chest, already. He ought to go to sleep. It was very late. His father had told the story of his conversion to-night and it took a long time. David had sat out in the front pew. "Let me tell you something," his father had said, "I'ma not got religion, and I'ma not got theology, I'ma got life, new life, not something put on outside." David said Amen. "Inside. Jesus give to me when I trust him, there in that li'l barber shop in Purvis, Miss'ippi, when I try learn a li'l English by read the Bible, look in dictionary every word, near 'bout."

He had told about being afraid to go into a Baptist or Methodist church because the floor was supposed to open up and devils take you down to hell. "I love the people in the Catholic church, God love them too, but I'ma tell you one thing, I don't need priest or some pope talk to God for me, I talk to God myself, you talk to God you'self." Amen, David said. "I don't call any man father but my own father, live in Sicily still. God is the Father, not somebody in a collar turn 'round, say hocus pocus you don't even know what is. Listen, I don't wanta be call reverend, li'l peanut like me. You calla just plain Joe Canzoneri, or Brother Joe, or craz' mutt, maybe you want to."

Other people kept saying Amen, too; the pastor and old Brother Nutt and some of the deacons. Afterward everybody crowded around his father and kept telling him that it was the best sermon they'd ever heard, but his father would say, "Well, that's not a sermon, just try to tell my experience with the Lord." David stood by, nodding. When nearly everybody had gone, David grasped his father's hand and looked straight into his eyes. "Brother Joe," he said, "the Lord moved me tonight like I have never been moved since the day he saved me."

"I 'preciate you give up you time to preach," his father said.

"Not at all. Not at all. No sermon of mine could ever be as dramatic as the way you tell of your conversion. Not at all. Not at all."

Go to sleep, he told himself. But things kept coming into his head, like the young bluejay Herbert had shot out of the chinaberry tree, lying there with black glassy eyes, feet folded. Think about something funny, he told himself.

The only thing really funny all week happened the first night. After the song service and the offering, his father had said, "My wife go to school here, high school, you see. Boarding school. Then go down to Hillman College, where I meet her. And you know something, we get married right here in Lena. We come over from Standing Pine, on eleventh of July 1918, and Brother Nutt marry us. So this ver' special place to me, glad to be here."

Everybody looked around at Brother Nutt, and he nodded

a little, like taking a bow. He was very old and hadn't preached for a long time.

"Now I gonna sing a solo, one my favorite song I hope the Lord use." When his father glanced at the pianist and she started playing, the boy tried to sit farther down in his seat. People said his father had a beautiful voice, that he could have been in opera, but lately all he could hear was the wavy sound running through it. Vibrato, his father called it. And he would sing each word separately, to get the message across, holding onto a note so long sometimes that the pianist would be left with her hands high above the keys, waiting for him to go on.

> I am a poor wayfaring pilgrim,
> Wandering through this world below.
> There is no sickness, toil, nor danger
> In that bright world to which I go.
>
> I'm going there to see my father,
> I'm going there no more to roam.
> I am just going over Jordan.
> I am just going over home.

When the song was over, nobody even fanned for a minute, although it was a hot, still night. His father stood and let the sound all die out, then he bowed his head and started to the steps down to the front pew, where he always sat and listened to the sermon. But Brother Nutt stood up and said, "Joe?"

His father stopped and looked out into the congregation at him. "I heard my grandmother sing that forty years ago," Brother Nutt said, "and she beat you all holler." He sat back down. His father laughed about it later, but then he just stood there with his mouth open.

Preachers, he thought. If they were right and if there was only one right way, then shouldn't they all be just alike? When God called them to preach, why didn't he make them perfect?

Make them all like the Apostle Paul or like George W. Truett, in Dallas, that people said was the best one now. His father had worked with Dr. Truett a long time ago, and he had written the boy a letter congratulating him on being born. His mother kept it in the box with the pictures. Maybe preachers ought to be what his father called scholarly, like Dr. Purser, the one who gave him the nickname Kerflumox that only his father ever called him. Or maybe quiet and gentle like Dr. Lovelace, who was dead now. The boy had seen his coffin let down in the ground. He jerked his mind away from that. Some of them were funny, he thought, like Dr. Patterson, who went hopping and gulping at the air in the middle of a sermon, saying some people were like a pullet chasing a grasshopper. He and Billy Rogers had laughed so hard they got down under the pew, and his mother had to pull them out.

He turned over on his stomach, put his head between the sheet and the cool underside of the pillow. The funny preachers didn't bother him, but some others did, like the one who had been at Hickory when they were; and then when they went to hear him at a revival in Jackson, he told exactly the same boiled okra jokes. His favorite song was "That Will Be Glory for Me"; he'd have the congregation sing it while he whistled the tune to himself, rocking from heel to toe.

David. The day they had chicken pie for dinner he wouldn't let the lady cut into it. "I can hit the gizzard every time." he said. He dangled his fork back and forth over the crust, stuck it through, and pulled out the gizzard. Everybody laughed but the boy was not sure what to think about it.

He heard his father come into the room, heard him getting a coat hanger out of the closet. He moved his head from under the pillow and rolled over.

"You not asleep?" his father said. He sat down on the edge of the bed. "You know, son, I think I tell you about Baptist World Alliance meet in Atlanta, and I like to go, but cost too much? Mist' Davis want to pay my way, he say, want me to go. Preachers from all over the world be there."

He roused himself. "Dr. Truett?" It was the only thing he could think of to say.

"Dr. Truett, R. G. Lee, everybody. Preachers from all different countries in the world. I try to tell Mist' Davis he shouldn't do that but he insist."

He tried to imagine preachers from all over the world. The nearest thing to it he had ever seen was the convention last year at the First Baptist Church in Jackson. He and his friend Atley had stood in the wide vestibule just to hear the preachers come out and blow their noses. "Why do they sound like that?" he whispered after one preacher had given a long honk—like something his brother might do on his trombone—then folded his handkerchief over, and honked again. "I don't know," Atley said, "but if it hadn't been so much I'd have thought it was his brains." He nearly died before they could get outside and laugh. It still made him want to laugh; so why, he wondered, did tears fill his eyes and spill down across his temples?

"Son? What's the matter?"

He could only shake his head.

"You be all right," his father said. "It's ver' late. You go sleep, we talk about it tomorrow."

The Book

The next day they had dinner at Dr. Lyle's house and were supposed to stay all afternoon, but his stomach began to cramp, and his father said, "I better take him back to Mist' Davis, let him lie down."

"He can lie down here," Dr. Lyle said. He was a dentist, not a medical doctor. "We've got plenty of beds."

It must have shown on the boy's face that he did not want to stay, because his father said, "I s'pect he feel better there."

And as soon as they got to their room and his father pulled the bedspread down he was crying again.

"I declare, son. Can't you tell me what's wrong?"

He shook his head. He did not know either, not all of it. That morning after breakfast was cleared away, his father had spread out his timetables and studied them for a long time. Finally he said, "Look like no way to make it if I go home first. Have to go on to Meridian and make connection with Southern to get Atlanta on time." He picked up his coffee cup, put it down, looked at the boy. "You think be all right to ride down Jackson by you'self? You be on Rebel. You mother meet you at the station."

He had not answered. He had never been anywhere by himself, and the thought of it scared him.

"I have to leave early in morning. Mist' Davis take you to train couple hours after." He waited again. "If I go." It would be his only chance; usually the World Alliance met in foreign countries, his father had said, like England and Brazil.

He licked his lips. "I want you to go," he said.

His father rumpled his hair. "That's the ticket."

He turned away, his jaw tight. " . . . go brush my teeth," he managed to say, and hurried upstairs.

In church that morning he had kept touching the pew, pulling his fingers slowly away from the thick varnish to feel the pull, the letting go, the lingering invisible residue. Anywhere he touched, a detective could sprinkle powder and see the lines and whorls that were like nobody else's in the world.

"Whatever you do today," David was saying from the pulpit, "is written minute by minute in the Book of Time forever. And when you come before God Almighty in that last judgment day, you will see it whole, like a story written, like a map of where you've been, like a moving picture used for God instead of the devil, flashed up on a screen as big as the sky. Your dark, secret, sinful pleasures will shine out bold for all to see—your lust, your greed, your gossiping and backbiting, your selfishness and pride. And, oh, my friends, do you realize you hang over an open pit of eternal fire and damnation?"

David stepped to the side of the pulpit stand, held up a hymnal for everybody to see, thrust it out in front of him like a platter. "Only God holds you safe, as I hold this book. Only the mercy and forgiveness of God sustains you. Oh, you may be held so high, my friends, that you do not feel the awful fires of hell leaping toward your feet. But they are there. Fire and darkness and eternal torment. And once it's too late, once God lets go, you will fall endlessly into the pit, never, never, never to return. Never, never, never to reach the bottom, my friends, because God is the only foundation and without Him there is nothing."

He stood holding the book, sweat beading on his forehead. "Falling forever, lost, burning with unquenchable fires through the long endless night of eternity. And God will let you go, my friends. God will let you go. Unless you trust him now, God . . . will . . . let . . . you . . . go." For a moment David stood motionless, and then the book hit the floor with a sound like a shot.

After the service, the people lined up to shake David's hand. "Powerful sermon," an old man said. "Powerful."

The boy stood close by his father; he felt that he could still hear the slam of the book, the reverberations through the whole church.

"We're going out to Dr. Lyle's for dinner," the pastor had said finally. "We can all go in my car."

They had walked down the aisle and out the door. When they stepped into the blinding sunlight, David slowed down to let the older men walk on ahead. "How'd you like that?" he whispered. "I really turned that ole songbook loose, didn't I?"

The Known World

"We s'posed to go back for supper," his father said. He could not say anything. "I declare, I don't know what to do with you, son. You cry last night. I bring you back from Dr. Lyle's, you cry all afternoon. Don't have fever, I don't think you sick. I go craz', you keep this up."

He lay there looking up at the light fixture, a glass bowl with faint white flowers all over it. If he concentrated on that, he could be quiet for a while. The light was not on. When he would glance aside at the venetian blinds, he could see strips of green where the tree in the front yard was, and strips of blue diminishing above it.

"Got to take the car back, anyhow." His father stepped over to the window, and the blind made bars of light and dark across his face. "You say you want me to go to Atlanta, but I guess you don't want stay here, do you? Don't want go home by you'self." He was silent a moment, looking out toward the tree. "Is that what the matter is?"

He cleared his throat, but he did not know what to say, even if he could talk.

"Don't you think God take care of you?"

The only thing that would come into his head was his Sunday School teacher telling how she prayed when her chickens got out and God helped her find them.

His father turned to him, shook his head. "I thought you big boy now."

He tried to say that he wanted to be, but his throat knotted up. He could see exasperation in his father's face, in the way he took a deep breath and pressed his lips tightly together. He flopped himself over and crammed as much of the pillow as he could into his mouth, into the sockets of his eyes. He heard his father let the breath out with a hollow sound, a sound that seemed to come from the gray puffed cheeks and rounded lips of the North Wind drawn on some old map of the known world, with its warped chunks of land and its blank expanses of ocean where legendary monsters swallowed those who might otherwise sail off the edge.

"All right." He felt the bed sag as his father sat beside him, felt the strong hand on his shoulder. "Daddy not goin' leave you. We go home together."

8 *Doors*

On December 7 we were at my Uncle Arden's house in Jackson; when the symphony was interrupted with news of Pearl Harbor, I watched the color drain from Aunt Vera's face and wondered why she turned pale. Didn't everybody know we'd go into the war before long? I had just turned sixteen; I was sure I'd never make it into uniform. All the fighting would be done by the thousands in khaki who had for months been passing down Highway 80 in endless caravans of army trucks. We'd sit in the front porch swing and watch them, the way we often watched funeral processions pass slowly westward to the cemetery just down the road.

In January my father drove us to the pastorate he had accepted in Kentucky. From the back seat of the car my younger brother and I watched the landscape grow bleaker as our house and our friends diminished behind us. The needles of the pines drew in and darkened, the oaks lost their tenacious clusters of brown leaves; along the streets of towns we passed through, black-limbed maples took over from elms, houses narrowed in upon us, flattened out in front, huddled closer together. Knobs like little mountains appeared as we drove into Lebanon Junction and the smell of coal smoke. The snow was black with soot, the buildings dingy. A drab man in a faded overcoat watched us pass his street corner.

In honor of our coming they had had Mr. Jim Mattingly fix the hot water tank, which was attached, in full view, to coils in the little coal-burning stove in the kitchen of the pastorium. Mr. Jim had a garage up the street with a yard full of torn-down cars. He'd come speeding down in his early-thirties Chevy, as loose-jointed as he, and swing the corner toward town looking as if the doors would come flying off, the way his elbows looked as he dashed about wildly at whatever he was doing.

My father was the exact opposite of Mr. Jim. He would not think of sawing a board without measuring three times. No matter how hard I tried, I was never able to mow the pastorium lawn near enough to his satisfaction that he did not stop between house and study and say, "Not like that, son. Here. Let me show," and finish the small back yard in his demonstration of what to my undiscriminating eye was precisely what I had been doing.

One Saturday night a year or so later, while I was on leave from the Navy, my mother sent me out to the study to help Dad with the church bulletin. "He'll be there all night," she said, "and he's got to preach in the morning." I had taught him how to cut stencils and operate the little hand-turned mimeograph machine. When I opened the study door, he was lining up a sheet of paper with great care. He cranked it through sharply to keep the ink from blurring, examined it all over, pulled his metal tape measure out a couple of inches and checked the margins all around. "Let me finish," I said. "You go get some rest." He did let me help, finally; I stood there half the night holding the ream of blank paper from which he lifted a sheet at a time.

Mr. Jim came to replace the bad pipe alongside the water heater before we arrived, while Dad was there alone, unable to say to this member of his new church, "Not like that. Here, let me show." The Chevy slid to a stop at the back gate; Mr. Jim leapt out and began throwing stuff into the back yard;

pipes, pipe threader, blowtorch. He dashed into the kitchen, glanced at the water tank, dashed back out, lit the blowtorch and set it down, cut a length of pipe, threaded both ends, rushed inside with it. Dad casually turned the blowtorch so that it wouldn't set the wooden house afire and went after him, met the screen door slamming wide open and Mr. Jim coming out with the pipe. "Too long," he said, kicking the blowtorch back around so that it wouldn't sear his leg as he cut a couple of inches off the pipe and threaded it again. Dad eased over to the blowtorch and managed to alter its direction as Mr. Jim turned to run the pipe indoors, circle in the kitchen, and fling himself out again, kicking the blowtorch back, cutting the pipe another couple of inches, threading it. This time Dad got the blowtorch around and made it to the door in time to see Mr. Jim motionless for a moment, holding the pipe up alongside the water tank, where it still overlapped the joints by an inch or so. He grunted, threw the pipe across his knee, and jerked a kink in the middle that must have hurt my father's sensibilities every time he walked into the kitchen all the years they lived there.

Most of what happened in that house I know only second-hand, but I was there when my father returned from Uncle George's funeral—the only time I know of that he went back to New York—where, he said, he had been forced to contain his own grief or the family would have gone to pieces. He no sooner walked into our house than the phone rang and some-one asked him to go up the street and tell a young woman that her husband had dropped dead at work in a baggage car.

I was away when Uncle Cyrus and his family came by on their way to California, when his daughter was there for a visit, when his son and bride stopped by on their honeymoon. I also missed the two Sicilian relatives whom my father had not seen for who knows how many years. One day, without warning, Joe pulled into the driveway between church and pastorium, got out of the car, unlocked the trunk, and helped

Ciro out. They stayed for two weeks, and then Ciro climbed back into the trunk and Joe drove off.

What got my parents out of that house after a dozen years was my father's illness. Some of the deacons came to visit and found him huddled against the coal stove in the middle of the dining room, the only warm spot in the house. Move two steps away in any direction, and you could feel the cold wind blowing through the walls. The house had been soaked up to the ceiling for two weeks during the '37 flood. They built a new pastorium, of stone, across town high above flood level, and my father ended his years as pastor in a solid house with an automatic furnace in the clean, dry basement, and a wood-burning fireplace in the white plaster living room. He methodically rolled newspapers as kindling, placed the logs with absolute precision so that they would draw well and burn long.

When he decided to retire, he was seventy. My younger brother drove a rented van up from Mississippi, and we spent New Year's Day of 1957 packing my parents' furniture to be hauled back to the house near Clinton. Everybody knew Brother Joe. He would be called on to do some revival meetings and supply some pulpits; he would work in his garden and prune his fruit trees.

A couple of years earlier I had taken a job at Georgetown College, and I went to Kentucky to look for a house for my wife and two children. The real estate man who showed me around for three days was an ex-tobacco farmer who operated out of a second-floor office with blank windows facing the courthouse. The faded plaster walls were bare, the wood floor was bare; the small coal heater, battered desk, and two or three cane-bottomed chairs were like a dry oasis in the vast desert of the room. After one of our excursions about the small town, he led the way into the office, threw his narrow-brimmed hat onto the desk, and sat down. "Add some figures for me," he said. He reached into his shirt pocket and pulled out a scrap of paper. We had just stopped by a house he had contracted to do improvements on. He called out numbers; I jotted them down. "Okay," he said. "What does that come to?" When I told him, he laughed. "Well, lost money on that one too."

On the morning of the second day he took me to a house he thought might do. "Never shown this one before," he said. He checked the beams in the basement, felt the wood with his fingernail, looked over the furnace. "She's asking twelve-three," he said. "But this house isn't worth that much. More like eleven-five."

We stopped by the owner's dress shop in town. "I've got a man here who might be interested in your house, but not at twelve-three. That's more than it's worth."

The woman huffed up like a robin fluffing its breast feathers. "What do you mean?" she said. "You're working for me, and you'll ask whatever I say."

"Not me," Everett said.

"*I* decide what the house is worth."

"And I won't sell one for more than *I* think it's worth," Everett said. "Here's your key." He tossed it to her and walked out.

"The one you want," he said that afternoon, "isn't really for sale. Old couple in it, retired from farming. But I just got this other house on the market that'll be better for them. He wants more garden space." He had been leaning against the wall, and now he rocked his chair forward. "Come on."

It was a low frame house with a porch and swing. Everything was painted, clean, neat. The old lady answered the door, the old man right behind her. "Come on in," she said. Overlapping scatter rugs made paths through the house wherever shoe soles were likely to touch.

"You remember that place I showed you down on Clayton?" Everett said. "Well, it's just come up for sale. I figured that if you wanted it, this young man might want your house."

"Well . . . " the old lady said. She showed me around, ran

her hand down the varnished door facings. "Your wife wouldn't need to scrub these down more'n once a week," she said. We went out back and looked at the cherry tree, the grapevine, the stand of raspberries.

Back in the house, the old man called me aside, led me to the door between kitchen and dining room, swung it halfway open, stopped it. It hung there, motionless. He stepped aside for me to swing it myself, feel the balance. Then he leaned over and said as though confidentially, "'Em's some of the finest doors you ever seen."

Everett drove me back downtown and we went up the stairs to his office. "Right about now he's saying, 'The tomatoes'd do better with that extra sunlight, over on Clayton,' and she's saying, 'It's a bigger living room, and we don't need a kitchen this big.' " Everett leaned back in his chair, brought the brim of his hat down on his forehead almost to his nose. "And he's saying, 'It wouldn't be no problem, him moving right in, like that.' " He sat there a minute. "About nine o'clock tomorrow morning he'll come walking into town. They don't have a phone or a car. And he'll say, 'All right, we'll do it.' I told him eleven—even for you, and that's what he'll agree to, because that's what it's worth. He ain't greedy like that woman this morning."

"It's sure the best thing so far," I said.

"When you come to leave, I'll get your money back for you. If I can't, I won't take a commission."

He had told me the day before how once he had needed some money desperately, and when the banker told him no, he went berserk, told the banker, "God damn you, don't you see I need this for my daughter and I'll get it if I have to choke it out of you?" And got it. Now he sat silently for a moment and then said, "They talk about crazy. Why, you could be sitting here sane as can be, counting your money, and somebody walk past that door and throw a stick of dynamite under your chair. Hell, you'd go head first through that wall getting out of here, plaster busting all around your ears. And that's crazy." He rocked forward, put his elbows on the desk. "Sure, everybody's sane long as everything's all right."

The next morning at nine the old man came shuffling around the corner as I was going into the doorway. I waited and walked up the stairs with him and into Everett's office.

Down in the half basement of that house I learned to stoke and bank the furnace by hand, and I tried to make wine from the grapes in the back yard, watched it bubble away in a stone jar; but it came out so sharp you couldn't drink it. During the two years we were there the door frames seldom if ever got washed down, the raspberries took over the garden space, we never got around to covering the wallpaper in the bedroom with its garish red roses. Still, the floors looked fine even though they had been walked on, and the doors kept their balance.

My mother and father had hardly moved back to Clinton Boulevard when I got an offer to teach at Mississippi College. At the time my sister was in Nigeria, my older brother was in Texas, my younger brother was getting ready to go to Brazil. It seemed up to me to be close by.

Everett began looking for a buyer, but nobody showed up. One day not long before we were to leave, he stopped by the house. "Let's sit in the swing," he said, "so she can see us."

"Who's that?"

"Lady across the street, three or four houses up, in the little dormer apartment. She can look right down on us. Keep her thinking."

"She interested in the house?"

"Crazy for it," he said. "But stingy as all hell." He settled back, put the swing in motion. "She and her husband built this house when they first married, thirty-some-odd years ago. Hardly got moved in when one of them's mother got bad sick, and they went off to take care of her. Now they're back, just the two of them and a little pug-nosed mop of a dog, sitting up in that little room looking at their house."

"But she won't buy it?"

"Probably put three, four thousand in it back then, and now it's worth eleven. It's hard for her to swallow. And anyway, she won't buy it through me. She's got a suspicious mind. Right now she is staring at the back of my neck thinking, what's he up to?"

"What are you up to?"

He grinned. "If you want to go on and get rid of the house, tell her you'll by-pass me and save her some money, and she'll snap it up. Two things there she can't resist."

"Lower the price? How much?"

"Tell her you'll drop it $250 and not pay me any commission. Not charging you one anyway, but she don't know that."

"Is that what you'd do?"

"Yeah. You'll need the down payment down there, and it'll cost you that much to hang on long enough, anyway."

"All right," I said. "I'll call her tonight."

He got up. "She'll call you back before noon tomorrow." It was eleven o'clock the next morning when the phone rang.

That was the eighth of some twenty-five houses or apartments we were in and out of, in Mississippi, Kentucky, Tennessee, Michigan, Alabama, Louisiana, California, Indiana, Texas, Ohio. All that time my cousin Nino and the others were settled in at Palazzo with no notion of going elsewhere—except when the earthquakes of January 1968 destroyed some nearby towns and the stone walls of Palazzo began to crack, so that they spent five days in the snow on the mountainside. "My sister cried," the younger Carmelo told me, "but I took it like a man."

Some people from Palazzo continued to come to America, however, and some of them occasionally returned. In 1971 my wife and daughter and I spent three weeks in a house just down from Nino's. A heavy wooden door opened to stairs, at the top of which was a large room on either side, each with a tiny balcony out the front window. One room opened into a small kitchen and a bath. In the rooms below, Nino stored his wine and olives. The house belonged to one of his in-laws who had moved to New York, but wanted to keep her house in Sicily.

One day when I had squeezed the Volkswagen camper up to the door to unload it, after a trip to another part of the island, we were approached by three men. One came forward, speaking English; the others hung back.

"Americans, aren't you?" the man said.

"Yes, we are."

"Me too. California. I grew up in this town, and so did my wife. She's coming in a couple of days. Both of our mothers still live here. God, it's primitive, ain't it?"

A couple of days later I was crossing the piazza, a sheaf of paper in my hand, and a car pulled up in front of me. It was the same man. He looked all around, leaned out the window and whispered, "I'm going to Palermo to meet my wife at the airport. Not going straight there, though. I don't trust these people."

I had just bought typing paper at the little tobacco shop and newsstand.

"Quanti fogli?" the woman had asked.

"Oh, maybe a hundred, if you have it."

She had gone to the stack of paper on the counter, but now she just stood there. Her hands made little indecisive motions. "Cento?" Somebody came in, and she rushed over to wait on them. "Un momento," she said to me in passing.

The hundred sheets seemed to stagger her mind, but eventually she got them counted out—thinner and tougher, longer and not so white as bond back home—calculated three different ways, accepted money. The next time I was in to buy stamps, she said apologetically, "Scusi, but when you bought the paper I made a mistake. I charged you for a hundred sheets, but I gave you a hundred fifty."

"If you don't need them, I'll just pay for the extra."

Her eyes were glazed. "Either way," she told me.

The story I was writing would hardly take a hundred fifty sheets, but we still had a long time to spend in Europe. I wrote in longhand on a clipboard, sitting on the little balcony with barely room for the straight chair, catching whatever sun got through the springtime clouds. My daughter, Nina, would be reading on the other balcony. When I finished for the morning, we would walk up through the piazzetta to Nino's for coffee, dodging chickens, nodding to the people in the doorways along the narrow cobblestone street who stared intently and without expression into our faces. Later my wife would struggle with the Italian keyboard of the Olivetti I had bought in Palermo, get onto thin paper the page or two I'd done so that I could revise it next morning.

I had not known when I began that the story would be written as if it were about other people, but would really be about us during the long years when Sicily had no more bearing upon our lives than some mythical island. Nor did I know that it would be a glance backward through some of the finest doors, foot poised to step out the last one:

9 The Little Kingdoms of This World

Night broke into morning with a snap, as if his mother's fingers had snapped a bean, one snap on one bean of how many dozen; another short green segment tumbled into the pan. The tail end of some song rose and faded into the heavy voice of the local news commentator. He opened his eyes.

The world was red. Morning light through the thin red curtains struck a bright rectangle on the far wall and left thin red dye in the air. With a sound like a frog leaping into a pond, the coffee began to percolate. Snap, the clock-radio had said, and it was morning. His wife would not open her eyes until the coffee was ready, but it was becoming morning for her too, gradually, darkly within her lids.

" . . . the story reached this reporter only yesterday . . . ." The voice was weighted down with import. " . . . the power of an incorruptible press. . . ."

Another snap would shut that fool up, he thought.

His wife threw a leg and an arm across him. You know how I hate alarm clocks, she always told him; I have to wake up by degrees. There was no music at this time of morning on any local station.

"Local," he said. He laughed, bouncing her thigh on his

stomach. "Did I tell you about Judy Wharton? They ran one of her commercials and the next day the girl at the cleaning shop said, 'I saw you on TV last night. I said to myself, Is that network? And then I watched it for a minute and I said, Naw, that's local.' "

She squeezed him and said something without opening her lips.

He nodded. "So I had told you. Learn to live with it. It has become, like all I meet, a part of me."

The room was a cube of red, the coffeepot plugged away inside, the commentator kept turning upon himself like a toenail growing in. Local. The single segment of a bean among segments of beans. He must have been dreaming about his mother's hands. Or had his mind transformed sound into memory, so that its walls would not realize they had been breached?

"Coffee's made," he said. "Loose me from these sweet bonds of flesh and let me pour."

"My lunch in here?" He opened his briefcase and looked. It was there: brown paper bag and thermos.

"What?" his wife called from the back of the house.

"Nothing." He shut the briefcase. The heavy sheaf of un-graded papers depressed him. "I'm off. Bye."

"Wait." She came into the kitchen. "You've got to go see Miss Smith, remember? And don't forget the kittens on the way home." She kissed him. "Have a good day."

"Yeah," he said. "Sounds like it." He had forgotten both things. It meant driving instead of walking. It meant getting to the campus half an hour later, which didn't really matter. It meant coming home too late to relax as much as he liked be-fore dinner. "Well, all right. I hope your day is glorious, too." She had already fixed breakfast and sent the kids off to school. She had been making up beds when he interrupted. Next she would get out the vacuum cleaner.

When he pulled out into the street, he could see where the path vanished into the tall pines. That was usually his favorite part of the day, that green half-mile walk to the campus. The path circled small apartments for married students. A dog with its leash on a clothesline would bark alongside him the length of its run. Some days a small boy would hurry out to the cedar that marked his bounds and talk through his allotted territory to the resinous pine. The boy's father was in the sophomore literature class; he always hung around after the bell, sweating with the exertion of thought, trying with small eyes to spy out some secret passageway through the uncomprehended mass of the course.

The elementary school was an angular enclosure of dark brick. Walking the empty corridor, he saw roomfuls of children reading, talking, stirring about. As he passed a wall plastered with paper American flags, the smell of paste took him back to his own third grade: Miss Cochran like a block of ice telling Richard Walton, "You're just a big baby. Shame! Shame! Eating paste at your age!"

Miss Eunice Smith was more like a shriveled pear than like a block of ice. She came without a change of expression to stand in the door with him, as if upon the tight immobility of her lips depended all order.

"Your son daydreams," she said above a whisper.

"That's true."

"I thought you ought to know."

"Yes, I suppose so."

They stood in silence. The children were writing, thinking ostentatiously with eyes aloft. His son did not look at him. A boy raised his hand, watching Miss Eunice expectantly. "What is it?" she asked him flatly.

"May I sharpen my pencil?"

She contemplated the boy for a long moment, expressionless. "Well," she said finally, "I guess so. This time." The boy went to the pencil sharpener. "His parents are Episcopalian," she said. "But they do take him to Sunday School."

The yellow sign at the entrance to the college said YIELD. How long had he been at this place? Going on nine months, about time to give birth to something. Maybe he himself was the embryo, ready to issue forth. There were kickings and stirrings, all right, that he had gradually become aware of. In the past few weeks he had been struck by a multitude of phrases, each of which left a spot sore to the touch. Only yesterday the dean had ended an interview by saying, "Of course you're right, but is it wise . . .?"

He circled the campus twice before he lucked upon a parking space. Bill Spencer, the economics professor, was backing out, shoving a pair of bumper stickers toward his vibrating car: Support Your Local Police; America: Love It or Leave It. Bill waved and sped off toward Beauregard Lake; he had complained mightily because he had to teach a morning class, leaving the bass to leap in solitude.

At the table where the faculty sat there was no one. He set his coffee down and pulled back a chair. The scrape of metal legs across the floor made about as much stir in the world as the usual professorial chorus of self-concern. Even now the petulant voice of Hank Franklin seemed to taint the air, like the stain of urine in old alleys:

" . . . and then his mother called up and pitched a fit; she's Jewish, you know."

He sipped the coffee. It was strong and hot, maybe the one thing here with those admirable qualities. Certainly he could not claim them himself. Nor could Nick, silhouetted in the doorway now, a gentle slope of a man, arms raised in greeting. "Ah, English! My own worst enemy!" Nick had published poetry in three or four languages, but had come to English too late and with too little energy. Why a Russian wound up teaching French and German at this remote college, no one knew. Religious connections, probably. Leading questions seldom led Nick anywhere. Now he came with his coffee and slouched into a chair, cut his eyes across the table. "You sit here how long?"

He laughed. "I refuse to answer your insidious question."

"Aha! You know you are wrong!" Nick gestured with both hands, clearing the air for his attack. "Why in English you say, 'I *have been* sitting?' No other language! English only! 'I have been sitting.' It means you quit."

"In English it doesn't."

"It means you quit. 'I am sitting here three hours' means you sit here while speaking. Why in English you say you quit when you still sit?"

He shook his head. "I suppose because we don't know any better."

Nick settled back and turned vaguely toward the bright glass doors. His face was thin and long, what used to be called aristocratic. They said he was trying to convince the dean that there was an error in his records so that he would not have to retire next year.

"I am sitting here not much longer," he told Nick. "I have a class."

Nick shook his head. "No other language," he said again.

If he had not heard a baby cry, he would have forgotten the kittens, forgotten the car, too, and walked home through the pines. It was strange to hear the cry of a baby on campus, and he did not know why it should remind him of the kittens. Perhaps all new creatures sound alike, he thought—except, of course, birds and reptiles and fish and pine seedlings. He looked around to see the baby, but no one was in sight. Perhaps it was in a corridor, waiting with its young mother for a thick sweating father to quit lingering in a classroom door.

The classified ad gave the address as 123½ on a street of small frame houses. Ned got out of the car at 123, uncertain what to do.

"Kittens?" It was a woman, standing beside the house, arms

crossed. Her sparse hair was pulled back; she had few teeth; her feet spread out through holes cut in tennis shoes.

"Yes," he said.

She led the way toward a small house at the back of the lot, dark beneath chinaberry trees. "How many do you want?" she asked without looking back.

"Two," he said, "if that's all right."

She turned abruptly. "Where do you live?"

"At . . . ." He pointed. "Over on the lake, just beyond the college."

"You teach up at the college?"

"Yes, I do."

"Well," she said, "if you teach at the college, you must be a Christian." She drew her lips in, studying him. "Are you?"

A moment before, he had told where he lived with unconvincing hesitance, he felt, uncertain whether to give his street address or a more general description. Now he stood hopeless, caught once more between definitions. In class this afternoon a boy had insisted, "Yes or no. *Was* Blake a Romantic?"

"Are you?" she said again, as if in accusation.

"Well . . . yes."

"And if you're a Christian, you wouldn't take those little kittens up there to the college and cut them up, would you?"

He laughed. "No. No. I should say not."

"Well, up at the college they do cut on them."

"I'm not in biology. I'm in English."

She turned then and led him to a shed behind the small house. "I have seven grown cats and four birds," she said. He could see the kittens stirring in the dark of the shed. "You teach poetry?"

"Yes, I do."

She hesitated at the shed door and then walked toward the house. "Come on in." She opened the screen and nodded for him to step into the kitchen. "I write poetry, myself," she said. She took some sheets of stationery from beneath a yellow canister. "I wrote this one yesterday. I can just write and write." She began to read. "The Snow."

The poem described snow; the beauty of snow, the joys of snow. She stopped abruptly in the middle of a page. "I could just go on and on," she said. "I think it would be nice in one of those Christmas books, with all the pictures, don't you?"

"Yes," he said. "I think it would."

The kittens worked out just right; his son took to the striped one immediately, and his daughter to the black one. "Keep them away from the road," he said. "We don't want them run over." He had told the woman that he'd take good care of them, that there was very little traffic around the lake. It was a good place to live. The house had glass across the front, over-looking smooth lawn, a narrow road, a sloping bank of grass and pine trees, and the lake itself. Now the sun was low in the trees, and the still water reflected sky and clouds. The children were close to the house, playing with the kittens. The striped one would rise on its hind feet, box his son's finger swiftly, and then leap away.

"I give him a month," he said.

His wife looked at him. "You're very cheerful."

He shrugged. Maybe it was only the time of day, but he felt as if he could see it all in advance: the kitten limp in his son's arms: He's still alive, isn't he? He's not dead? He would take the soft fur. I don't know, he would say. He would cover the kitten with the little blanket his daughter had used in nursery school. When the kitten was stiff, he would bury it in the empty lot back of the house.

The scene was so vivid that even when the kittens were safe inside and the children asleep, he could not get it out of his mind. He and his wife sat in the dark and looked out over the lake.

"What is it about water?" she said.

"I don't know." The moon shone through thin clouds,

defining the lake as a flat ellipse, vaguely disturbed, ragged at the edges with dark trees. The houses on the other side sent quivering streaks of light toward them. Earth, air, and water. The lake seemed alive, mysterious, contained. "Maybe we see ourselves in it."

"Like a mirror."

He yawned. He was not sleepy; it was just that she had irritated him, stating the obvious, making him sound as banal as he was. "I'm going for a walk," he said.

She got up. "Let me check the children first."

"I'll be by the lake."

He leaned against a pine tree in the dark. She had not noticed that he said, "*I* am going. . . ." And surely he had not meant that they saw themselves in the lake as in a mirror, face to face. If anything, he must have meant that looking as if into the water they saw only their own small portion of sky, their moment of a passing cloud, their neighbors' lights shaken by intervening pines. He had not really seen the coming death of the kitten any more than he could see what lay deep within the lake. He had only caught reflections of what had been, of what was. Everything seemed to reveal itself by boundaries, as glints of light off one facet or another. He himself he knew mostly as others glimpsed him: in turn father, husband, teacher, representative of the English language, fetcher of kittens. You must be a Christian. Are you?

Except that there was life pulsing out from within and in from without. He could feel it, could feel the threat to the skin which held him together, to the invisible membrane containing what he could feel, what space he could fill with blind concern.

A sudden breeze across the lake shattered the long runners of light for a moment, and as they drew together again in diminishing loops, he caught a dark, brief silhouette.

"What is it?" his wife asked, beside him now.

He must have started. "Nothing." It had been only an old

snag, one he had noticed many times before. But more than once this spring he had seen the head of a water moccasin gliding erect through the surface like a finger upraised in warning.

10 *Reflections*

As one apparent result of the visit to Palazzo Adriano with my father in the fall of 1969, I began writing stories out of my childhood. Always before I had avoided autobiographical fiction, and I had long ago given up on mirrors. Perhaps the perspective of Sicily made me want to draw back and watch my past take form, to discover if possible the shape revealed by whatever glints of light had touched upon the space in the universe peculiar to me.

The following spring, unexpected violence on campus shook my assumptions enough, as I see it now, to turn my attention to the present as it contained configurations of the past, the significance of which I sensed only as patterns. I did not suspect as I wrote, that late summer of 1970, and did not realize until after my life turned from what had seemed a predictable course, that part of the texture of the story came from undercurrents flexing like muscles just beneath the surface:

Gulf

When with mask and snorkle he would lie on his face, the rocks and shells and tiny darting fish underneath him became his world, although he breathed the separate air. He could

turn over and be in air invisible as water, under clear blue sky
or high-piled clouds, near his wife and son and daughter
partly in sight and partly submerged beneath the reflective
surface.

Certain memories would recur as if he were to turn and
discover them underwater, clear as in liquid, seen from above.
They would linger, inviting him to see into, through, beyond
them, as if warning him that not to divine their substance
meant for the rest of his life to live without knowing either
how or why.

During an evening in Ohio three such memories came to
him, reviving other memories, so that he wondered if somehow they fit together, unrelated as they seemed. The scenes
remembered all had taken place in Gulf states—whatever that
might imply—the first in Florida, somewhat farther out to sea
than his shallow-water snorkeling.

Gulls gathered over the mild Gulf, some distance ahead,
dipping and wheeling in the soft air. Beneath them the surface was intact but discolored, darkened, like a bruise coming
under translucent skin: sardines. High above the gulls invisible jets made thin incisions which immediately scarred white
and began healing back to unmarked blue. The old man said
that deeper than the school of sardines, Spanish mackerel
would be following. He and his young son and the old man
rode the surface in a boat, trailing the mackerel.

He managed, as usual on his rare fishing excursions, to
catch nothing. The old man caught two and, when they
turned back toward the bay, motioned him to let the boy have
a try. Haphazardly, far from the sought-out school of sardines, the boy caught two more mackerel. The old man slit
the fish easily with his sharp knife, lifted long pale filets. That
night they broiled them with lemon and butter.

Many years later he asked his son if he remembered the
week in Florida.

"Of course. The mosquitoes nearly ate me up."

He himself would have given anything to go to Florida,

when he was a boy. The nearest he ever got was a family trip to Biloxi in the Model A, and he still could feel the cool Gulf night and see the phosphorescent water at the tip of the oars, on the way to Deer Island and a bonfire, with wieners and marshmallows. His children would not eat wieners, but to him they had always been a treat, as going to Biloxi was, as was driving to his grandmother's even—the only place they ever traveled, it used to seem.

"There too," he told his wife. They were having their second martini—their only indulgence, they thought of it as—and their son came out the door.

"You going to need your car?" He pulled a comb from a tight pocket, looked at it, stuck it back. The jeans he insisted on wearing had holes at the knees with frayed thread. His hair was long and thick.

"What's the matter with yours?"

"I don't know. The brakes are acting up."

"Well." He sipped the martini. Sun was in the treetops at the edge of the yard, and he could feel the first touch of fall in the air. "I was just about to tell your mother that we are the deprived generation. My father's car was *his*, and I couldn't get it. Now, I provide my son with his own car, and he takes mine."

His son laughed. "You were just about to tell her that," he said. "Sure you were."

"Well, actually, about how we used to eat at second table when we went to my grandmother's. The adults ate first, and we ate whatever was left."

His son had one foot off the patio, easing toward the garage. "Should have sneaked into the kitchen ahead of time," he said.

"But your generation? We always fed you kids first, and we ate what was left."

"I won't be long," his son said. "Back in time to eat."

"You'll notice," he called after him, "that we've had second table all our lives."

From an upstairs window his daughter asked, "Where are my curlers?"

"You don't want to do your hair now," his wife said. "It's nearly time for dinner."

"My *electric* curlers."

His wife sighed. "Where you left them."

"Where are they?"

"On your desk, I think. You've probably covered them up with dirty clothes like everything else in your room."

The footsteps going away from the window were unduly loud.

"She can make me so furious," his wife said.

"Well . . ." he said. "Maybe she'll grow out of it."

"I don't know. But I think maybe you'd better talk to your son."

"My son?"

She nodded. "He'll come nearer listening to you than to me. He says we've always treated her better than him. He says she gets everything she wants."

"That's nonsense."

"I know."

"How could he possibly believe that?"

"And he's been fooling around with drugs."

He turned to look at her. The leaves of the shagbark in the distance stirred in a breeze he could not feel. The sky was clear. He felt that just beyond his ability to distinguish was the smell of ripening hickory nuts. "How do you know?"

"I don't. But he acts like it."

Questions swarmed just in sight, just out of reach, but he chose to focus on one nearer at hand, one he could twist wryly against himself: "But where would he get the money?"

The Trees

Another memory, of Mississippi, also tantalized him with its clarity and persistence, not altogether because of the sky, although since he had lived in Ohio blue had assumed increasing importance. There were many days here when, driving up High Street, he could not tell whether the fog had been wiped from his car windows or not: the world looked the same either way.

But that day in Mississippi was a fresh spring day, a day when, perversely, every living sensation was a shock of pleasure. Standing in front of the house where he had grown up, he watched three jets mark a sharp geometric pattern on the blue. Accidental, surely: only from that one point in space at that one moment, moving on as the planes inexorably were, could it be seen as he saw it. He was between the hospital, where his mother sat with her dying mother, and the house he and his wife and children had recently moved into. He had taken his grandmother's soiled clothing home to be washed; returning, he had stopped to speak to his father. While he was there, he soon learned, his grandmother died.

Irony, he could say, but only because irony—which was obviously not what haunted him—was all he could name. His grandmother had decided, at eighty-six, that the washing machine did not get the clothes clean, and so she turned over the old iron pot, built a fire under it, and was hauling water two buckets at a time—she would not even use a hose—when she was stricken.

Her clothes were still warm from the dryer. His father shut off the mower and they talked of how the grandmother probably would not last through the day. Earlier she had squeezed his hand, her own more bone than flesh. When he left the hospital, she was unconscious, rasping long breaths through her hollow mouth, caved in at the cheeks, gaunt. When he returned there would be only the still ridge of her face, and then they would put her on a cart and pull a cover over her, and she would be gone.

The trees had long been gone, but he could never get them out of his head. The front yard had been terraced down to the road, and his father had made his whole two acres, except for the garden, into lawn. He stood now, small and straight, with one hand on the mower handle, dripping sweat.

"I ought to help you with that," he told his father.

"Oh. I enjoy it," his father said.

Years ago the yard had dropped off abruptly to an abandoned roadbed grown up in sage grass. Across the front edge of the yard and beyond on both sides oak trees had stood in a line. The biggest tree was hollow; it blew down one night when a hurricane came that far inland from the Gulf with such howling force that, although they were awake, putting out pans to catch water blown under the roof shingles, they did not hear the crash of the tree. He could remember it down, seen out the living room window next morning, could remember the disbelief, the shock, and then the laughter of his older brother because he was crying; he could remember saying, "But I *liked* that tree."

He had liked each tree—one for climbing, another to play beneath with tiny imaginary people—but especially he had liked them all, the sequence of them. As his grandmother died he was standing where the old hollow tree had been. What had happened to the others he did not know, but he could feel himself aligned with them; as if they were still there, as if by stepping on that spot of lawn he had taken the old tree's place in line, as if the world were using him to try to make itself complete again. At that moment everything was clear and sharp, verging on some ecstacy of realization.

Toward the Sky

When he had finished the second martini and had eaten the olive, he said to his wife, "Well if he's away till dinner and she's rolling her hair, why don't we be extravagant and dissolute? I'll mix another drink."

"Lots of ice," she said. And, later when the sun was gone

and dusk diffused itself under the trees, "I like this time of day."

"So do I," he said. She was in a canvas chair, just out of reach. He put his hand out toward her and she took it. "I like you."

"I'm afraid we like martinis, too," she said.

"It's no longer fashionable," he told her. "We'll never be the avant-garde."

She shook her head. "I was thinking about your mother's letter."

"One came today?"

"I meant to give it to you. She says your father is showing his age, and he wants to put in a bigger garden, but she's having to do most of the work on the one they have now."

"Well, I suppose when you get up into your eighties. . . ."

"But he's still keeping the lawn. Oh. And what I started out to tell you is that she said some couple in the church there are having trouble, and then she said, 'He drinks, you know.'"

He laughed. "Another little dig at us."

"Only we're not having trouble."

"Right." His parents would never understand them, really. Now his salary was five times the most his father had ever made, and he'd saved nothing. His father had loaned them the down payment on their first house, and they had always lived on credit: Enjoy it; now is when you're living. "I sometimes think that deep down beneath their caring for us and wanting everything good for us they halfway wish that we'd suffer for our sins, just to prove them right."

"Maybe we will," she said. Tears welled up in her eyes and she brushed at them with her hand.

"Sweetheart," he said. "What is it?"

"Oh, I keep worrying about the children."

"They're not bad, you know."

"She never cleans up after herself and gets mad if I say anything."

"All girls her age do that."

"And he's so . . . directionless."

He squeezed her hand. "Well. I was too. I still am."

She looked away, looked up toward the sky, which was still an aching blue. "Don't ever leave me," she said.

Ghosts of Light

"I'll do the dishes," their daughter said as they ate. She was dark and beautiful, so that he always wondered how she could be other than happy. She turned to her mother. "I'm sorry," she said, obviously about the curlers.

"What's bothering you?"

"Oh. Nothing really."

"Well," he said, "your hair does look good."

She began to laugh, pointing at him. Her laughter had always been infectious, irresistible.

Finally he said, "Now what the devil are we laughing about?"

She shook her head as if he were hopeless. "I decided not to roll my hair," she said.

His son looked up from under the hair fallen across his forehead. He had good eyes, straight at you, clear, blue. "You heard the new Dylan album?"

"No. I don't think so."

"You've got to. I'll borrow it." A car honked outside. He stood up. "Well, bye."

After dinner he and his wife took a walk. They liked where they lived, it had both trees and plenty of sky. The neighbors lived their own lives and did not intrude upon one another. Others were walking; they spoke briefly and moved on. As they were returning home they saw the moon rising in the trees.

Something woke him in the night. He lay quietly, listening, but all he could hear was his wife's breathing, a distant plane, trucks on the freeway whining faintly, a dog far off. It must have been something in his own mind, a memory, a thought, or just this sense of unaccountable joy.

Briefly, when their daughter was less than a year old and their son about three, they had lived in an apartment in Alabama with a complex of doors at the center. He awakened one night to find his son standing at the bedside. It had happened before; he had to rouse himself and lead him back to bed.

He stumbled around in the dark for several minutes before he finally stopped. He could see the faint outlines of windows through doors he could not identify. For a long time he stood, holding his son's hand, in a senseless world of dark and tantalizing ghosts of light.

"Son," he said quietly, "do you know where we are?"

"Sure."

He had let the hand pull him along, and in a few steps the house had begun to line up again.

The Center of It All

The moon was past its height, shining in their window now, laying its own bright rectangle diagonally across the fainter white of their bed. The window itself was another rectangle of light. He felt that he had the pieces in his head; lying quietly there he could will them to move into symmetry, to become a single straight-sided figure: the sheet over his wife's body and his own, the transparent glass, the light itself.

He lay motionless. Beside him he could see the form into which his wife molded the sheet. How could so known a shape move him to desire and pleasure time after time? Why was he happy, simply lying here beside her? I was being foolish, he would have to tell his son; ours is not the deprived generation.

The first time he had seen her asleep was when he took her to meet his parents, and up in the night, as he drove through heavy fog, she put her head in his lap. They had hardly known each other, then, and there she was, trusting him, off in a white nowhere, her head in his lap, asleep. He took a deep breath. How often since had their son and daughter slept the same way. He lay so upon his pillow, now, the sheet upon him, the moonlight upon the sheet.

There were so many things he had never said, so many that he could never understand enough to talk about. It was as if he were the single mind of the world, the only perceiver, as if when he grew into consciousness the world began and when it came his turn to die the world would end. As if he alone saw to the periphery of vision, he alone saw complexity, immensity. But he knew that when he spoke it was all too simply, as though he saw only a single focal point. Was that true of everyone; or was he really the center of it all? As he lay here, now, did the entire universe turn upon him, a hemisphere always beneath him and a hemisphere above him? He could feel that it was so.

But when he thought of his wife, a few inches to his side, he could feel a minute shift in the massive universe. It would, he found, move intact to his son's room, his daughter's. Had the old man in the boat perceived in the Florida scene a different set of layers? What of the jet pilots, with the boat and birds and fish reduced to nothing, unseen, unthought-of? Did each gull, each sardine, each mackerel feel himself to be the fulcrum, the delicate balancing point of all existence?

The window and the bed had not moved, but the moonlight had. Soon it would reduce from rectangle to line to nothing. But only for him. The way the house stood, moonlight would be increasing now in the room of his son.

We are where we are, he thought. We are what we are. He knew that he did not understand, that he would never see it whole, but for now he felt that the hints were enough. His wife turned toward him and he put his hand on her gently. Lying here, he loved her and the scenes of her life. He loved his son

A Highly Ramified Tree

and what the world was only to him, his daughter and her life to its periphery. Trust them, he wanted to say to his sleeping wife, to himself, to his son, his daughter, the neighbors he hardly knew. Trust us all.

11 Relics

It is unlikely that my father would ever have returned to Palazzo if it had not been for admirers he never met, Pep and Polly Pepinsky, who lived just down the street from our house in Ohio. I had told them so much about my father that when I mentioned, during the summer of 1969, a tape of him telling his life story, they were eager to hear it. The voice rich with Sicilian had been rolling along for only a few minutes when Pep stood up and declared, "I want to send him to Sicily." In that instant, we knew what we should have known all along, that Sicily was not the mythical place it had seemed, but soil and rocks surrounded by salt water; the town my father had left was of palpable stone. He had to go back; I was the one to take him; it had to be very soon.

I had little notion what to expect there, but I settled into the long lazy September days in Palazzo Adriano as if I were born to them. At mid-morning, a couple of the men would awaken my father and me at the little albergo; we'd dress and follow them across the street, drawing in the clean air, admiring the deep blue sky. My father would be reminded of "the old song Caruso used to sing"; they'd urge us into the bar through the doorway hung with heavy plastic strands; they'd order espresso, unwrap apricot-filled cakes, refuse our attempts to pay: "No. No. You are our guests."

We would be taken one day to Antonietta's, the next to Nino's, the next to Giuseppina's, to sit in cool rooms while the women fixed dinner: soup, pasta, a veal dish or tough little snails called babbaluci, wine, fruit, nuts, cheese. "Mangia, mangia!" Marietta would say without looking up from her plate. For the first few days I would struggle to eat all the pasta while they tried not to tap their forks impatiently. Before long I was putting away the entire meal with the same loud gusto as my cousins.

Then, "Riposo. Riposo." Two hours of sleep in a shuttered room before we would drive into the campagna; to the lake; to Bisacquino, with Tina and Giovanna and Felicina singing "Che bella la Sicilia" as we wound our way back along the mountainside in the early night; or to Chiusa Sclafani to buy shoes from Antonietta's cousin, and then to visit above the store in a parlor with heavy drapes and with cattails in a bronze vase. For help in translating cattail into Italian, I turned to Giovanna: "Come si dice l'ultima cosa d'un gatto?" How do you say the ultimate thing of a cat? That sent them into laughter; they had only smiled when I entered the shop and, confusing volere and volare, announced, "I fly some shoes for my father."

Back for supper. At Giuseppina's it would be soft-boiled eggs and leftovers from dinner, served yet another floor above the more formal living-dining room. We would go through an ancient kitchen, kept much as it had been for perhaps centuries before the recent addition of electricity and bottled gas, and sit at a round table in the large room with Pippo's desk and bed. Two floors down, Giuseppina's husband, Carmelo Alessi, showed us a clean stall with a caged rabbit, a furry little donkey, and the mule he rode to the campagna and back every day that he was not obliged to stay home and entertain relatives.

One afternoon he got out a box of photographs and dealt them onto the table, saying, "Tina and Pippo in the country," or, "Our friend the dentist with his wife and children." When he came to a postcard picture of a statue of Santa Teresa, he said, "La sorella di mia moglie," and watched to see what I would do. "Your wife's sister," I repeated. He nodded. I picked up a card with a picture of San Giuseppe: "And this is her brother?" When Carmelo laughs, his mouth is like a great cavern; he slaps your shoulder to be sure you're aware of his appreciation.

This Carmelo had more English than most of my relatives: "AT'S enough! (Significa 'Basta,' non è vero?)" and "Oh YES! (Significa 'Sì'?)." When I returned some eighteen months later, in April 1971, a couple of English phrases had been added. His wife, Giuseppina, would shout at odd and distracting moments, "You shut up, you!" and go helpless with laughter. And one evening Carmelo, enduring on the verge of sleep the talk of the womenfolk, leaned over and rasped in my ear, "Gawd damn."

It was hardly enough English to serve, so that in the after-supper gatherings of the family, one of the younger folk would square off and begin talking to me in very distinct and deliberate Italian—no one expected me to master Sicilian—and I would respond as well as I could. Soon, building upon what conversation we had groped into, we would be saying anything that came to mind. At midnight, when my father and I were there, the men would take us out among the other men of Palazzo to stroll arm in arm through the piazza and down the broad tree-lined Viale Vittorio Veneto. At the heavy wooden door of the albergo, they would tell us goodnight. I'd turn the iron key in the lock and we'd climb dim stairs to our room.

"Intellegente," they would say of me at first. "In three days he will speak Italian perfectly." Soon it was "in eight days," and finally, "When you return in '71 you will speak Italian perfectly. Promesso?" And I, bravely and, as it turned out, falsely: "Promesso."

A Highly Ramified Tree

A certain hypocrisy of that time I tried to contain as neatly as Carmelo's animals were shut off from the immaculate marble staircase to the living room: I was able to dissociate myself neither from my father's attempts to evangelize nor from his abstinence. I told my cousins that I was—as I actually was for that brief period—under doctor's orders to drink nothing containing alcohol, but I felt that they surmised I would not have drunk their wine anyway. How could I say to them, with my father constantly at my side, that I never drank or talked religion in front of him? And if I managed to get that across, how explain my compulsion to relieve newly-found relatives of misapprehensions I allowed my father to keep?

It was my father's trip, I told myself. Why spoil it with revelations that could only hurt him? I would come clean in '71. That he might be suppressing some of his own feelings did not occur to me until we were on the way back to the States. In his "witnessing" to his nieces and nephews, mostly in English, he had avoided saying anything against Catholicism. But expecting him merely to see the sights of Rome was, I suppose, like expecting Carrie Nation to sit quietly by in Clancy's bar; he broke his silence, and I broke my resolution not to interfere with whatever he wanted to do.

My father's only interest in Rome was to see the catacombs and the Coliseum, where the early Christians had suffered. The Coliseum, according to a map of the city, was handy, but uncertain of the catacombs, I booked us for a tour without realizing that it stopped first at the cathedrals of Santa Maria Maggiore and San Giovanni in Laterano. The guide seemed to me irreverent enough, in his quips about the Church, to suit the most Protestant taste, but my father stomped around the periphery of the group muttering more and more loudly. When we boarded the bus after the second cathedral, I ventured to suggest that we see what we could and gather what information we could, and give voice to our disapproval later.

He spread his hands, palms up, rigidly in front of him,

clamped his mouth tightly closed; then he said, "It just make me mad, see all that gold, supposed to be spiritual."

"Well, there's a lot of history too," I told him. Normally, he would have been interested in history. "Like those doors that used to be at the Senate. Julius Caesar was killed in front of them."

He paid no more attention to me than he had to the guide. "The Catholic Church milk the people instead of serve them; make a big show."

"Whoever got milked for that gold is long past our help."

"They enslave the people and use them for their own purposes."

"All right," I said, "but we just found out that your nephew Nino spent three years in prison because of Mussolini, so why didn't you get upset at Mussolini's Terminal?"

"That's different."

"Well, what about the antebellum homes in Natchez, built with slave labor? You aren't indignant when you see them."

In the big bus seat, with the outskirts of Rome passing beyond him as on a giant screen, he looked very small and shrunken, but his eyes were fierce. "The Catholic Church do this in the name of the Lord."

"Everybody does everything in the name of the Lord." At least, I added to myself, in a manner of speaking. I turned away to keep from saying more. Here I was, spoiling it all, with only a day and a half to go.

Fortunately, our guide at the catacombs was a layman, whose account of the early Christians fit my father's concept so well that he whispered to me, "That's not Catholic doctrine; it's the truth. He better not let them hear him." He would look down the corridors of bare earth and expand with pleasure. "I declare, I just *see* those Christians, live down here true to their faith."

Next day, after he had envisioned them suffering and dying at the Coliseum, I ventured another suggestion:

"There's not much we can do on Sunday here, so I was wondering if we might not take a look at St. Peter's.".

"You want to see it?"

"Well, yes, I really do."

"All right with me."

He was on his best behavior. After admiring the Pietà, he stopped at statues all along the way, ignored the fact that most of them were of popes, and had only one criticism: "Who carved that statue?" he would ask. "They don't say who carved that statue." I steered him past things that might set him off—people fondling the toe of the bronze St. Peter, the confessionals, the entrance to the Treasury, where they charged admission—and we made it all the way to the altar and back to the portico without incident. There I noticed for the first time the booth from which guide tapes could be rented.

"Look, Dad," I said. "We should have used a tape. Maybe it would have told us who carved some of those statues."

"Had what?"

"Did you notice people with tape machines and earphones? Those are guide tapes. They rent them here."

He looked at the booth a long time, lips compressed; then he said, "I knew they'd be selling relics."

My father's return to Sicily in 1969 may have been almost as much a surprise to him and me as to our unsuspecting relatives, but once there, I could promise Nino and the others to return in 1971; a trip to Europe that spring had been planned for a long time. My wife and daughter and I would pick up a Volkswagen camper in Luxembourg, meet our friends the Coreys at Orly on Easter Sunday and travel together down through France and Italy; we decided to add three days in Palazzo Adriano before going on to Palermo, where the Coreys would take a plane home the first week of May; we would stay on in Sicily till mid-June, alternately in Palazzo and visiting other parts of the island, before heading back through Italy, to Spain, France, England, Holland, Germany.

On their last day in Palermo, the Coreys came down from their room in the Hotel Jolly for our usual lunch in the camper, of cheese and bread and wine. "Now," Irene said, "everybody has to name his favorite thing in the whole trip." We had been together for nearly a month, because of their particular interest in seeing late Romanesque and early Gothic cathedrals, mosaics at Ravenna and Monreale, theaters in Avignon, Vicenza, Taormina, and Siracusa.

Nina, my daughter, responded immediately: "Palazzo Adriano." She had chosen that even before her seventeenth birthday dinner in Siracusa, where the waiter had asked if she were a movie star, and in spite of the traumatic first night in Palazzo, when little Tina had asked me if Nina could spend the night with her and her sisters, and I responded, "Certamente," without considering that Nina knew no Italian.

Irene thought for a moment. "That's everybody's favorite," she said finally. "We'll have to say, other than Palazzo." In her long black cape, she had made a tremendous impression upon my relatives, doing sketches of them, quickly picking up enough of the language—as did Nina—to laugh and chat with them. One morning about dawn she went to sketch in the piazza. Only the street sweeper, with his long curved broom, and a carabiniere were out. When the sweeper moved into her vicinity, the carabiniere grandly gestured him away, apparently explaining that the dust would bother her. Whereupon the street sweeper went to the fountain, dipped in his broom, and very discreetly sprinkled down the cobblestones all around her.

Palazzo was my favorite, too, even though it was there that one painful aspect of the long trip was most intense. I would come clean in '71, I had promised myself. I had not anticipated a larger hypocrisy, an obsession which made every moment a struggle to present a normal face, to keep hidden what I could not tell my daughter, my good friends, the relatives I had deceived in what now seemed so minor a way about wine and religion. And a still deeper hypocrisy: I could not admit to my wife or even to myself that my infatuation with a girl half my age was not something I was going through, but was as profound and permanent a change as my father's conversion from Sicilian Roman Catholic to Mississippi Southern Baptist.

I felt removed from the fields bursting with wild flowers, the incredibly blue Mediterranean, the cloud topping a mountain near Erece like a perfect mushroom, as if I were seeing through old skin not quite sloughed off. But in memory the scenes are clear, as if who I am now saw them sharply, in sunlight and pure air, while with that wife and with the daughter who seems in some ways the only one to have survived as herself, that other person made his half-blind way about the island suppressing change until, or so it seemed, it translated itself into physical turmoil.

12 *War*

"Jesus!" he shouted. "We'll never get there!" There was another gurgle deep in his guts; his skin contracted, went cold, exuded clammy sweat. He clung to the steering wheel, hoping the spasm would pass before the next hairpin curve. "Toilet paper," he said through clenched teeth.

He heard his daughter lift the rear seat of the Volkswagen camper. "Here," she said, leaning up beside him.

His wife took the roll. "There's still no place to go," she said.

"The middle of the highway may have to do."

His daughter laughed. She began humming the Beatles song, "Why Don't We Do It in the Road?"

They were in a straight stretch with a foot or two of dirt beside the pavement before the drop-off. He pulled over as far as he dared, set the brake, dashed across the road and up the dry hillside through low thistles. The lone olive tree wouldn't hide him, but he got behind it anyway. His hands shook so that he could hardly unbuckle his belt.

Three more twists of the road, and his stomach was cramped again. He'd felt fine when they left the campground in Palermo, but on the edge of a little town he had stopped at an ice cream shop. His daughter loved granita limone. "You want some too?" he asked his wife. She nodded. The man showed him how he made it, pouring fresh lemon juice and sugar into an ice crushing machine; it came out almost as fine as sherbet. He decided he would try it.

"He has a brother in Brookaleeno," he said when he got back in the camper.

"Who doesn't?" his daughter said. "Mmmmm. This is good."

"Sure is," he said. A quarter of an hour later he was in agony, driving the Trapani highway with its towns and cleared fields and no place to hide. He had stopped at two service stations; one had no rest room, the other he had used despite its crusted filth. The little mountain road northward to San Vito lo Capo was shoulderless, bushless, nearly tree-less.

"San Vito, save me," he said as he finally drove into the town. A block of blank stone buildings, a couple of cars, docks ahead lined with fishing boats. Down to the right, the street followed the coastline as far as a church. He turned left, swung around a dark stand of trees and up the western rim of the cove alongside stone houses with rowboats tied to little piers. The road dwindled; beyond the last house he could see nothing but bare peninsula out to a lighthouse. He stopped. At Palermo they had said there was an excellent campground here, and the fish were delicious. "Christ," he said.

"You swear a lot lately, too," his wife said.

"That was a prayer."

A man carrying a bucket came out of the house and crossed the road. He leaned out the window. "Prego, signore, c'è un luogo per campeggiare vicino?"

"You can camp right here," the man said. "Fine place."

"Grazie. But I want to find the campground."

"I'll bring you water, and I have a restaurant. Excellent food. Right through that door."

His belly growled. He gripped the wheel tighter. "Maybe," he said. "But I'd like to look at the campground first."

"It's back at those trees. But it's dark there. You have plenty of light here."

"Grazie. Forse ritornerò." He turned around.

The trees were clumped together in a large circle, too close to get the camper in among them. Two old men were sitting on a bench nearby, where a few low plants seemed to outline vague paths. "I'm going to see if that's the rest room," he said. It was a small brick building near the trees. The door was on the other side, heavy weathered boards. The padlock rattled when he shook it. His legs were jerking spasmodically as he went back to the camper.

"What are you going to do now?" his wife asked.

"Disgrace myself, likely." He drove the half block back into town, climbed down out of the camper in front of a little shop. A couple of men were leaning on a Fiat, talking.

"Scusi," he said. "Do you know where the campground is?"

They looked at him blankly for a moment. Finally one of them pointed across the street at a boarded-up building. "The hotel is there," he said, "but it is closed."

"Non voglio un albergo. Campeggio. They said in Palermo there was a campground here."

The man looked at the camper. "You sleep in that?"

"Yes."

"You can go up near the lighthouse and camp anywhere."

"But. . . ." He struggled against the fresh onslaught in his guts. "Gabinetto? Where is a W. C.?"

The man shrugged. "Use the rocks."

Back past the restaurant the road became a pair of faint tracks on bare rocky soil; huge gray boulders formed a long sea wall. He rushed down among them, leaping from one to another like a frantic mountain goat. The camper was a white block on a vacant landscape; when he glanced to see how far he had come, the top went up, like a bellows distended, an in-drawn breath. Back in town a motor started and settled into a slow putt-putt-putt. At last he found a little hollow of rock, a drying tide pool open to the empty bay. He nearly tore his zipper out as a spasm hit him. His hands shook so he could hardly grasp the sides of his pants to pull them down. Another motor started; the first one, he realized, had grown louder, was on a fishing boat now throbbing into view, a man in the stern, a woman at the prow. "Son of a bitch," he said, jerking his pants back up.

The boat glided past, putt-putting like the gristmill near his grandmother's house when he was a boy. They must be going out to check some nets, he supposed. Before they got out of sight, the second boat hove into view. He sat on a huge rock, felt its rough erosions with trembling fingers as he watched the entire fishing fleet go by, one by one. When the last boat passed going out, the first one was coming back into his line of vision, headed in.

That night he was hot with fever and he ached in all his bones. When the first chill wracked him, his wife said, "Shouldn't we get you to a doctor?"

"None here, you can bet." His teeth were chattering so he could hardly speak. "Even the hotel is shut down."

"Well, we could go where there is one."

"I can't drive."

"I could try it."

He shook his head. He could hear the low waves washing against the rocks. There was no moon. He shut his eyes, shut himself within himself, hot as he was. Why did the sickness strike him and not his wife and daughter? Maybe it wasn't the granita. Maybe it was just time, the way volcanoes and riots and wars reach the moment of eruption. The way boils rise beneath the skin, come to a head, burst. The way pimples sprout on adolescents, and middle-aged men suddenly go berserk.

"This is the second time you've had this," his wife said. "It may be partly in your head."

"In my head?" He knew what she was talking about.

"Not wanting to be here."

"I'm here," he said.

He kept his eyes shut, his knees drawn up with his arms tight around them. His wife clung to him, bruised as she was, aware as she was that as he had driven down the Rhone Valley white with pear blossoms, to Venice and Fiesole and Rome, to Sicily orange with poppies, he was seeing it all as through a gray veil, aching, enduring. And, yes, suspending himself in a kind of numb terror, perversely afraid that at some turn of the road his vision would clear, the ache subside, and he lapse into being as he had been for their twenty-one years together: sane, respectable, happy, neither suffering nor inflicting pain.

"It isn't fair," his wife whispered.

"I'm sorry." He grabbed the flashlight from under his pillow. "Got to go."

There were not many lights back among the houses. He crouched in the dark, listening to the sea. The stars over his head would be over the girl's head about six hours from now. A dog was barking somewhere in town. The sound was hollow, as from a dry well. His insides felt hollow, too, for the moment, his guts flat, flabby, empty.

When he stood, pulling up his pants, it was as if he unscrewed from the earth half a turn, so that he straightened facing west instead of east, into the smell of the South China Sea instead of the Mediterranean, into a time as distant as the place was: a quarter of a century ago, pulling up his dungarees with this same gut-empty feeling on Mindoro, the plane a dark hulk in the early light. Could that really have been the same person as the one now torn between a wife, as yet unknown to him there in the Philippines, and a girl, then yet to be born? Had the sloughing off of his old cells so many times made him as new as his son had been twenty years before when he raised his head up in the nurse's arms, straight out of the delivery room, looked him square in the eye, and let out a squall? Before that, a blank, like a hole in the air, a vacancy nobody knew existed until he filled it, and then his not being was unimaginable.

Or like the inside of a pot, not there until the clay enclosed it, but a presence from then on, if only in the curve of its ancient shards—the way a person left evidence of himself in his clothes, his books, his house. A coffin, a grave, a stone with receding dates carved on it. Bones, at the very least, mingled as they may be with others in a charnel house, lost at sea, burned to ashes. A voice, a shape in somebody's memory.

Back on Mindoro, his crew had been assigned to go through the effects of a crew whose plane had gone down, and he had come across a single hint, a fragment with the slightest inside surface, and still after all these years kept the imprint of a boy he had never known. Most of the things clustered around the vacant cot he had resisted so that he no longer remembered them, but when he picked up the dead boy's diary it fell open at a description of a smell that had haunted him too, and that he had mentioned to no one.

They would cross the South China Sea at 10,000 feet; fifty miles off the coast of Indo-China, they would drop down close to the water, the smell of sea strong after the high thin air. He would squeeze into the tail turret, sit between the big fins of the Liberator, watch the blue sea unrolling beneath him. Soon he would know that land was close, could see the water shallowing to brown, could smell the parched earth or thick forest before it slid out from under him. Sometimes there would be a different smell, like incense, perhaps, or some fragrant plant: sweet, pungent, unmistakable. He would try to make out what it came from, perhaps the trees with clusters of orange flowers, although sometimes he smelled it when none was in sight.

As much for the dead boy as for himself, he had tried to search it out, later, when he caught a whiff of it in the amusement park at Long Beach. It was in one spot near the roller coaster, a small pocket of aroma hanging in the air head high. He could walk into it and out of it. He went to the shop nearby and sniffed every perfumed candle and every spiral, cone, stick of incense, while the little Chinese woman at the cash register watched him. Finally he said, Would you come smell something for me? She looked uncertain, but followed him outside, through a dozen yards of air disturbed by screams from the roller coaster, saturated with popcorn, cotton candy, harbor smells. It was still there, separate, intact. Here, he said, stand right here. Obediently, she took his place. Smell it? She shrugged. On tiptoe, he said. Nose in the air. Now? She nodded. What is it? She shook her head; I don't know.

His stomach was roiling again already. He sat on a rock and waited. No need to go back to bed just to jump up and run again. The air was cool on his feverish skin, and he shivered, gritted his teeth against the chill coming on. When it passed, he was left shaking the way he had been after the bomb went off in his face. What happened back there? the pilot had asked, and for a while he couldn't answer because his thumb wouldn't stay on the mike button. Instead of dropping beneath the plane and coming into view as it lodged in the railroad bridge or bounced off the tracks, and instead of delaying three seconds after it hit, this bomb came loping back end over end right under his feet, fell slowly away as the plane lifted over the trees, exploded before it reached the ground. A chunk of it tore through the plane a few inches behind him, right through the metal stool you put a waxed paper bag in if you had to shit. He had to again now, here on these indestructible Sicilian rocks.

Where was it all coming from? He must have unloaded—how would you measure it—bushels, gallons, barrels? Maybe so many litres or kilograms, here. But he had eaten only toast and jelly for breakfast and the one cone of granita since. On Mindoro it was always pancakes that did it. His crew would be awakened at four in the morning, go yawning and stretching down the chow line. He could never resist the pancakes; they were better at least than the mush of powdered eggs. On the way out they would pick up a big box of C rations and another box with a chunk of roast, loaves of fresh bread, and big cans of grapefruit and pineapple juice, enough to feed the dozen of them for up to fifteen hours in the air. They'd go back to the tent for earphones, parachutes, flight jackets, climb onto an ordnance truck and be driven to the plane. By the time they got their gear stowed, it would hit him. He'd lunge up through the after hatch, grab the big knife from the survival kit, and saw feverishly into the heavy waxed box of C rations. Inside there would be four separate boxes, and he would slash them open one by one until he found the toilet paper, swing down through the hatch, dash madly off the hardstand jerking down his dungarees. Afterward, weak and shaken, he'd go back to the plane and walk the propellers through.

Funny that the act of pulling up his pants should have brought the war back so clearly; he hardly ever thought about it now; once it had seemed that he would always identify himself in relation to it, like the old man at the Confederate reunions when he was a boy. The dwindling group of Veterans gathered every year under the cedars by the old Chapel. Slaves had made the red brick; the chapel proper had been used as a hospital for Union wounded back in 1863, and Grant's horses were stabled in the classrooms underneath. Outside those windows, surrounded by boys, one old man would level his walking cane: This is the way I shot Yankees: Bang, bang, bang. When the ladies tried to serve him coffee in a china cup and saucer, he would wave it away. Get me a tin cup. Drank it that way during the War and never drunk it any other way since. Past the gray old soldier he could see, beside the watermelon-red crepe myrtles at the college entrance, a real cannon from the World War squatting between spoked wheels thick with gray paint; the heavy barrel sighted a silent trajectory out over the town.

He had never dreamed back then that he would be sitting here on the northwestern tip of Sicily, looking out into the night over an island of wars, a chunk of land everybody had sent warriors to: Phoenicians and Carthaginians, Greeks and Romans, Saracens and Normans, Spaniards and Austrians and Germans, even the English and Americans. Where he grew up, he and his brothers would sometimes find spent arrowheads, where Indians had skirmished with early white settlers, he supposed, and miniè balls where Grant's army had shot its way through to Vicksburg some seventy years before. Then, that had seemed the distant past. Since, he had looked between Greek columns 2500 years old at the ancient city of Agrigento, modern now, a pleasing pattern of balconied towers replacing the rubble of Allied bombing.

At the next onslaught he thought of Etna, even now spewing lava on the opposite end of Sicily, himself matching her eruption for eruption, as if to keep the island in balance. When he rose, the sea wall was unsteady beneath him. He braced himself stiff-armed against a rock, let everything drain out of his head, held there until the blackness dissipated and consciousness seeped in like slow clear water in a well. On his way back to the camper a fresh chill shook him so hard that he dropped the flashlight, stood quaking in the dark a long time before he dared lean over to pick it up.

He awoke to sunlight, the buzz of a small car passing just outside, the fresh morning gurgle of his guts. He grabbed the roll of toilet paper and opened the camper door. Farther down toward the lighthouse a little Fiat had stopped. People poured out, stacking up sticks and branches as for a bonfire. Before he could get to the sea wall, two more cars sped out from the town, careened toward him, swung off beside the camper as if in a parking lot. More people. More sticks and branches. A man began unfolding a table. From the docks came the putt-putt of fishing boats on their way out again.

He turned back to the camper. "Let's get out of here."

A spasm hit him as he let the clutch pedal out, and the camper lurched toward the sea wall. His daughter was letting the top down. "Ouch," she said. "You don't have to break my neck."

"Goddam Sicilians," he said. "All the space in the world and they have to wad up in a little knot."

He fought the steering wheel around, pulled onto the faint tracks. The dark stand of trees was surrounded with cars; he swung around it and sped through town as fast as he dared. All along the road little Fiats were pulled off in every tiny space flat enough; families were sitting around white table-cloths, eating, pouring wine. In Trapani, the service stations were closed and all the buildings were blank with heavy steel shutters like garage doors pulled down over the shop fronts.

The campground at Marsala was across the road from the sea, walled in with stone. The men's room was clean and private; there were no other campers. He rested awhile on a lawn chair under the locust trees. "Let's cruise," he said to his daughter finally. "We've got to find some food for tonight."

At the entrance, he backed up to let a car turn in, a small Mercedes with a loaded rack on top. An elderly couple; blond; undoubtedly German. The sun laid a blinding path toward him. He turned down the coastal road, took the first street into the town, drove between shuttered shops. "I hope our gas holds out," he said.

"Is that open?" His daughter was pointing to a steel front lifted partway up; the sign above it said Alimentari.

"Better try it," he said.

They stooped into the dark store, made out a thin man perched on a barrel. "Buona sera. Si può comprare un pò di cibo—patate, carne, cipolle?"

"Si. Come vuole. Ma nienta carne."

"Why is everything closed today?"

"Feast day. All over Sicily."

"And you?"

The man slid off the barrel, shrugged, picked up a couple of yellow onions. "Make a few lire," he said. "Queste cippole? Ne vuole di più?"

The potatoes were on to boil when a police car drove into the campground and two uniformed carabinieri got out. The older one, mustached, courtly, led the way, bowed to his wife and daughter. "Buona sera. E benvenute a Marsala. Your trip has been pleasant, no? We hope you will enjoy your stay." He motioned, and the younger carabiniere handed him two fresh red carnations with long stems. "For you, bella signora, and for you, bellissima signorina."

" Thank you," his wife said. "How pretty."

"Grazie," his daughter said.

The carabinieri saluted in his direction, bowed again, walked across to the tent of the German couple.

"That was nice," his wife said. "Maybe it's a good omen."

He did not answer. The sun was so near the horizon that he could not see it beyond the stone wall. Right now it would be directly over the girl's head. Maybe she was crossing the campus, her feet wading in an ink blot of shadow. Maybe she was going now into the brick walkway between buildings down which only a year ago troops had faced defiant students, bayonets set, rifles loaded, hands trembling.

Suddenly over the stone wall of the next enclosure, a clear bugle call. He caught the movement of a flag beyond the trees, fluttering as it was lowered into the waiting hands of some soldier.

13 *Masks*

When I was in Sicily with my father, we were taken to see the farm he remembered as his sister Feliciuzza's dowery when she married Carmeluccio Glaviano. From among the olive trees, the figs, the prickly pears, we could see Palazzo on a spur of Monte Rose across the green valley. Inside the stone farmhouse, the older Carmelo Glaviano showed us the date 1928 on a wall with two names written above it in large strokes: these were men who had helped his grandmother Feliciuzza keep the farm going while for three years her husband and sons were unjustly imprisoned.

"In 1943, when the Americans came," Carmelo said, "I was spending the night in the campagna, sleeping in this room. I must have been—what?—ten years old?" He led the way outside, pointed up the steep slope to where he had left the car on the narrow shoulder. "An American plane dropped a bomb on the road, there," he said, "almost on my head."

Toward the end of that visit, we took time to see Agrigento. Standing on the beach at Porto Impedocle, deserted in the rain, the younger Carmelo and Pippo posed as I raised my camera. Beyond them in the shallows was something I could not identify, like a huge overturned concrete bathtub.

"Che cosa è?" I asked.

They shrugged their shoulders. "Non lo so," Pippo said.

Much later, having driven down through the mainland and seen pillboxes intact on mountainsides, looking slit-eyed out to sea, I would decide it must be a disabled relic of the last war.

We had spent two days among the Greek temples. Carmelo and Pippo had sat with my father and me in the car during the worst downpours, had gone with us through ruin after ruin. On the way back to Palazzo, I asked Carmelo if he liked temples.

"Mi piaccionno le ragazze," he said. "I like girls."

A few days before at Giuseppina's—she is the youngest of my first cousins in Palazzo—we were eating a dish of rolled veal; before us was wine for which her husband, Carmelo Alessi, had tromped the grapes himself. He was in from the campagna for the special day. He has a great expressive face, a cavernous mouth. He slapped me on the knee.

"Mangi com'un uccello," he said. "You eat like a bird."

"No. Mangio com'un porco," I answered.

He opened his mouth wide, guffawed with appreciation. Through the bedroom door I could see a colorful afghan on the foot of the bed. Tina, their daughter, had crocheted it; she had shown me several others upstairs, earlier, where Pippo slept and had his study.

"How do you make so many things," I asked her then.

"What else is there to do?" She was nearing thirty years old. She is, as my father said when he first met her, a very pretty girl. (I say it in English, he told her. I can't think of it in Italian. Pret-ty, we say in English. Pret-ty. Means beautiful.) She looked out the window, over rooftops of dull red terracotta weighted with stones to keep strong winds from lifting the tiles. "Here, all a girl can do is stay at home and help her mother, sew, cook, clean." Her voice was birdlike; her eyes were perhaps wistful for a moment, but then she turned and smiled. "So, that's the way it is."

"How would you like for it to be?"

"Oh, it would be fun to have un ballo, from time to time." I took out my pocket dictionary; I had been fooled before. But ballo turned out to be just what it sounds like, and I realized that I should have thought of the opera *Un Ballo in Maschera, The Masked Ball*.

In 1971, Antonietta is still in mourning for her husband, my cousin Sebastiano, but although she seems distracted and sad from time to time, she is always ready to go. Getting up the high step to the front seat of the camper is difficult, but she learns to grab hold and swing herself in as if it is nothing. "Always in the primo posto," the younger ones tease her, as she sits upright beside me, watching the road. We climb from the highway up the mountain into Prizzi, park the camper, go on foot through the narrow, steep streets, each looking down onto the rooftops of streets below

"You like Prizzi?" Tina asks.

"Sì, mi piace," I say.

She shakes her head, makes a gesture with the hand outward from under her chin. "Brutto. Brutto." I remember my father's saying that Prizzi and Palazzo used to be rivals, and sometimes there would be fights.

"Perchè?" I ask her. "Il panorama è molto bello."

She points to a house high above us. "Stupido," she says. "Look at that balcony." It takes me a minute to realize that it is built out from a window too small to step through, and its floor is scarcely three feet under the overhanging roof. "Useless," she says. "Stupido."

Antonietta becomes winded. She goes into a house—I cannot tell whether of friends or strangers—and sits in a straight chair to wait while we climb to where the cliff drops abruptly off the back side of town. By the time we get back to the camper and help her into her primo posto, she is in a state of nerves, face and hands twitching, little noises escaping her lips. I am worried, but they keep assuring me that it is not unusual; she gets this way from time to time.

Her daughter Felicina puts her to bed, comes back into the dining room where everybody waits. "Perhaps she will sleep," Felicina says.

For days everyone has been talking about the festa at Chiusa Sclafani; tonight at midnight the popular singer Nada will appear. She is about the same age as my daughter, they say, and looks like her; Nina must go see her. It is only today that I have discovered the girls have no way to go. Now I ask if they want to ride over with us. They are delighted. Tina and Nino's Felicina go home to get ready.

Antonietta's Felicina sits at the table with us. She is short and dark; she laughs easily, she loves fun. Now she tries not to look unhappy. "I can't go," she says. "I can't leave my mother."

"But, can't we get someone to stay with her?" I ask.

She shakes her head. "I have to stay with her."

Her aunts, Giuseppina and Nino's wife, Marietta, begin to talk with her in Sicilian. I understand little of the dialect, but it is impossible not to catch the drift. They are urging Felicina to go on with us and have a good time; they will stay with Antonietta. Felicina says, No, she will be upset if she wakes and finds her daughter gone. It is her duty, her place, to stay. Tears well up in her eyes. Ever since Sebastiano died, Antonietta has been this way—just waiting to die too. Sometimes she seems to revive for a while, as she has on our outings lately, but even then she closes in upon herself so that you have to speak to her more than once to get her attention. Felicina is over thirty. Who knows how long she will do nothing but nurse her mother, missing out on what there is of her own life?

"Figlia mia, figlia mia," Giuseppina and Marietta keep saying to her. "We will stay with her. Surely she will understand."

Felicina keeps shaking her head. "It is what is expected of me. It is my place."

Even Francesca's young daughters seem already to have their places. Little Giuseppina is the artist and writer and scholar. Little Tina is the homemaker—no less intelligent or talented, perhaps merely younger. Felicina's older brother, Carmelo, is the man of the house, the breadwinner. His younger brother, Nicola, is the married one, living nearby in his own house with Anna and the children. Concetta, the youngest of Antonietta's children, is in medical school in Palermo, where she has lived with her aunt and uncle since she finished elementary school with such promise. No one can understand how my son, Tony, can have chosen to stay alone in America rather than herd about in Europe with his father and mother and sister.

"It is my place," Felicina says, tears impossible to control. "It is my life."

I wish I had not brought up the festa, but the others are set to go, and Felicina will not hear of our staying on her account. Nada turns out to be, as they have said, young and pretty like Nina, but she looks less like her than Concetta does; sometimes when those two are dressed alike I get them confused, walking together down some Palermo street, or in the catacombs of the Capuchin monks all hung about with dried corpses. There, when we visited, Nina was startled by a monk who approached silently as she studied the distorted faces staring blankly from the wall. "She is very wise," the monk said. "She fears the living more than the dead."

Sometimes I feel more like the dead than the living, on this trip. I want to tell my cousins that the body they see walking around tyring to look as if it is alive is no longer inhabited by me. Its attempts to smile are no more real than the contortions of the dried monks along the walls of the catacombs. I am off in some sort of limbo halfway across the Atlantic, suspended between here and there, between whatever I have been and whatever I will become.

Palazzo itself, so little altered from my father's departure in 1903 until his return in 1969, has made its own changes in the eighteen months of my absence. Giovanna is married now, as planned, and since Nicola's Anna was heavily pregnant on my first visit, it is not startling that she has a child. But who could have anticipated this bright-eyed boy? He is named Sebastiano after his grandfather, but always called "SE-bastiano! Monello!" There's never a moment when he's not into something. New as he is, already he has a tiny sister, soon to be christened Maria Antonietta.

When my father and I were there, none of our relatives owned cars, and only one a television set; by 1971 there's a car and a TV at every household. The midnight stroll in the piazza now includes the women, too. "It has become acceptable for a young man to talk with a young woman," the younger Carmelo tells me, glancing through the throngs at the Chiusa festa. "But of course it still ruins her reputation."

I want to tell my relatives not to change, not to lose the charm of the old ways, the leisure, the pure air, the quiet. But they know both the danger and the advantages of the progress it is impossible wholly to resist, and they deal with them far better than I deal with the change in myself that I so dread and so fiercely desire. I hang on to the itinerary of the trip as if it were a guide rope around the rim of Vesuvius; let go even so frail a certainty and I may fall into the crater, or try some wild leap down the slope of barren lava.

In a cathedral back up in France, I found myself impatient with my friend Corey's lamentation over noseless statues. Those "vandals," I wanted to say, were attacking, not art, but symbols of their oppression. Long after the Coreys have left me in Sicily with my wife and daughter, the argument keeps running: Statues, customs, books, marriages exist not for themselves, but for our response to them; they are worth keeping only so long as they make our lives better; if thy statue's nose offend thee, cut it off.

A Highly Ramified Tree

I have said none of this to Corey, and I keep it inside all the way through Sicily, because I cannot yet face what it implies about the books I have worked so hard to shape, the marriage I have nurtured for so many years, the image of myself I have created by means of whatever reflections I could bear to look at.

Palazzo's festa will be in August; we cannot stay for that celebration, but we do manage to catch part of one ceremony and the aftermath of another before making our fractured way to Messina, Amalfi, Rome. One morning we are taken to the municipio and crowded into a big double room where the mayor—il sindaco—is making a speech. Soon he calls up one by one the dozen or so surviving veterans of the first World War, pins on a medal, kisses both cheeks. When it is Nino's turn, we strain to see. He has fought in both World Wars, has scars from each. On the front of the municipio are marble plaques naming the local dead from the two world wars; in each list there is a Giuseppe Canzoneri. Non sono parenti, my cousins have told me, but I am not sure how far they can afford to count kin here where families stay in one place for so many generations.

After the ceremony, anise cookies are passed around, and trays of heavy glasses filled with strong liqueur. I drink a sip at a time, as I would after dinner back home. As I am finishing, Nino calls from the next room. "Roberto! Vene cca!" I make my way him, standing beside the sindaco. They hand me another glass; we raise our drinks together; I try to do as they do, turn up the thick glass, gulp once, set it down empty. When we walk into the sunlight, the cobblestone piazza tilts under my feet.

I have met the sindaco before, although then I did not know what his position in the town was. We had gone to the Greek church for the christening of Maria Antonietta, but no one was there; we walked up to the house of Nicola and Anna. "Oh, the favors did not arrive in time," we were told, "and

Nicola has been delayed." The women and girls gathered around a table and wrapped candy-coated almonds in little squares of net, placed them in cups designed as white swans.

"What time will the christening be, then?" I asked.

"Nine o'clock tonight."

When we arrive at the church at nine, the doors are locked, the church is dark, the christening is over. We walk on down to the hall the older Carmelo has built and join the festivities. Carmelo organizes a quadriglia; I sit with some men I do not know. I tell one that the wildflowers of Sicily are the most beautiful I have ever seen. They are beautiful, yes, he says, but not as beautiful, even so, as those of Germany.

The sindaco comes to us, bringing the priest of the Greek church who, everyone says, looks like me; meeting him, I decide it is only that the beards are similar. He smiles blandly, sits, says little. The sindaco, a small man with quick dark eyes, begins goading him.

"He is very rich," he tells me. "The church has money put away it has no use for. But he writes letters to the Stati Uniti begging for gifts, saying how poor and desperate he is."

The priest's smile does not fade.

"You," the sindaco says to me, "you are a religious man?"

I shake my head. "No. Not religious."

"Catholic? Latino, o Greco?"

"No. I was protestante."

"Ah." His eyes are very bright. "You were protestante. Not any longer?"

"No."

"What, then?"

"Nothing."

"Niente? You do not believe in God?"

I shrug my shoulders.

"No intelligent man can believe in God, non è vero?"

I laugh, "I have many intelligent friends who believe in God."

"You are an atheist."

"No."

"You are a communist."

"No."

"You have never thought much about spiritual things."

"Oh, yes. I spent many years trying to understand."

He puts his hand on my arm. "When death is near, then you will believe, non è vero?"

I shrug again. "I cannot know that. Forse sì, forse no."

"You do not wish to decide."

"I cannot. It is not possible to know. For now," I tell him, "aspetto. I wait."

He has not taken his eyes from mine. Now he nods, whether in approval or merely dismissal I cannot tell. He turns to the man on the other side of the silent priest; they begin a spirited discussion in rapid Sicilian, hands flying. When the sindaco has made a point, he sits, eyes alert, listening to the response. Just as the other man seems on the verge of clinching his argument, the sindaco grasps his flailing arm and holds it still, choking his adversary into silence. I think of the old woman I have seen in Palermo with the rigid outstretched hand, of the desperation choked within me. In my head a surreal world is taking form; we will be ferried to Scylla from Charybdis and drive halfway up the boot of Italy before a bizarre encounter in St. Peter's releases it. I will sit beside the camper, parked among the pines of Rome and write "The Boot" on tough Sicilian paper. The words that follow will embody the shape of my silence as one of the old woman's thumbs resembles another.

14 *The Boot*

"You speak English?" she said. "Thank God for that."

Behind him the canopy of Bernini was reaching toward St. Peter's dome; his body was in a gentle corkscrew from having looked up a post of twisted bronze. Before him stood a slender British woman; her short gray hair was dripping wet. He put a hand to his own dome, touched his fingers to unanointed skin.

"I'm in an awful mess, you know. I was sitting out at a little tea room yesterday, and a carabiniere hit me over the head with his stick and tried to take my passport. I haven't an idea what to do."

"Really?" he murmured.

"Oh, he wasn't a real carabiniere, of course. He was just dressed up like one. They do that, you know, to take advantage of you. Like the priests and nuns. Many of *them* aren't real."

Off to the side, people kept doing something to their lips and breasts and touching the polished toe of St. Peter, who sat, darkly metallic, more upright than a straight chair.

"They stood up and shouted, 'Non è giusto! Non è giusto!' The English people did. And he ran away. I was reeling, positively reeling, so they put me in a taxi to the British Embassy, but of course it was closed. Saturday, you know. Closed today too."

"Sunday, yes," he said, polishing the toe of his shoe on the leg of his trousers.

She braced herself, as though the floor might roll. "Well, listen, mate, when my husband returns, there'll be war. He's in charge of the maritime, you know. A sailor, my brave Bob, with eyes as blue as the sea."

It occurred to him that his own name was Bob and that his own eyes were as blue as the sea. "Just call me Tommy," he said.

"I thought the thing to do is talk to the Holy Father. Don't you agree?"

"Yes. Yes, of course."

"But how does one get to the Holy Father? I've tried to find a priest, but do you know there's not a priest around? Not a one."

He looked toward the banks of wooden confessionals, toward the altar, toward the distant open door. "I don't see one."

"Why in Westminster they're all over. The place is thick with them. But here! It's very like the Italians. The way everything is dirty, the way they treat their wives—disgraceful. They don't care about their churches. They don't care about God." She gave a little laugh, looked off, fingered her glass beads. "They don't believe in him."

"There's a nun," he told her.

"They're useless. I tried to tell one of them my predicament, but she merely said, 'It seems unlikely.'"

His hand was at his throat. "I'd like to help you." He attempted a wry smile. "But this is not even a reversible collar."

She studied him a moment. "You're the wrong color, anyway, with those stripes in the shirt, and the jacket blue."

He turned his blue eyes away. "Tommy," he said. If he were not Bob and her husband were not Bob, he might have said Bobby. That might have reassured her.

"But how *does* one get in to see the Holy Father? What is the front door, so to speak? You'd think this would be it, wouldn't you?"

He gestured vaguely toward what seemed to be keys in the bronze hand of St. Peter. People kept touching themselves and touching the toe.

"He's here, all right. I saw him at noon, from the square. There were multitudes of priests around then."

He had been there too, one of the thousands of heads all looking up at the far window where the tiny white figure stood like Punch himself, arms waving so. Any moment Judy would appear, and, whack, the arms would have the paddle aside her head. When he spoke, the voice came large into the left ear, as if from the dome itself. When he waved, all the hands waved back.

Her fingers went to the wet fringes of her hair. "There's another entrance, of course, away off to the side, where one goes in to visit the Sistine Chapel." As if she had paused to let it, something began to occur to him; he felt prickles over the blank dome of his head. "But of course that's closed on Sunday." She gave a genteel little snort. "I say to them, 'If this were London . . .' And then I stop and say, 'But obviously this *isn't* London, is it?' Oh, it makes them furious."

He could say to her that it had all begun in Palermo— actually, back when they shot Jack Kennedy, but this time in Palermo—when he saw the old woman with two thumbs.

Two thumbs? she might respond. I have two thumbs, you have two thumbs, every person with all God gave him has two thumbs.

But, he could counter, both of hers were on one hand.

She would look at him for a moment before turning away. Over her shoulder, faint in the vast emptiness, the words would float: It seems unlikely.

Yes! he would call after her. Yes!

The girl at the Embassy was tall, her voice fit the room exactly.

Here in this corner of a foreign land, its tone implied, is a spot as American as a cube of ice is cold. The portrait of Richard Nixon behind her hung like a smudge which had tugged itself into definition, which clamped itself viselike even now to hold the tenuous outlines proper to a face. The girl seemed half humorously to ignore it. Presidents may come and go, but we unelected and unassassinated stay on forever. She handed him back his passport. "Your number," she told him, is K1221754. If you say 1 equals A, 2 equals B, and so on, it spells KABBAGED. I notice things like that."

"Oh?" he said, feeling his head.

"What can I do for you?" she asked. "Did you realize that you were born a day after Bobby Kennedy, rest his soul? He was thirty-eight one day, you were thirty-eight the next day, and the day after that his brother was killed."

He sat forward in the leather chair. "I'll be forty-six this year," he told her, "the same age Jack was."

"Yes, of course, I noticed. But, then, you're not the President, are you?"

His laugh seemed to him terribly unsteady. "Tommy," he said.

She shook her head. "Robert. It's in your passport, you know. I remember things like that. People call you Bob, perhaps? Bobby?" She did not wait for an answer. "But what can I do for you?"

"A tattoo artist." He licked his lips. "I want to find one."

"An American tattoo artist?"

"An artist," he said. "He must be an artist."

She reached for the telephone. "Of course. It happens that we are in touch with an American tattoo artist here in Rome at this very moment. He bills himself as the Tattoo King of the Western World."

He nodded. "I like a man who knows his limitations."

"Birra," the Tattoo King of the Western World said. "You want beer too?"

He nodded.

"Due birre," he told the waiter. He hitched around; the chair upon which he sat was enveloped in fat. "I talk a little Eyetalian. I know a lot of Eyetalians in North Beach. That's how come I'm here. One came back to the Old Country and showed this baron a saint I had done on his back, and he sent me a ticket. Wanted his coat of arms on each shoulder, but the son of a bitch died before my plane could land at Leonardo da Vinci. Ain't that a helluva name for an airport? Can't collect one single solitary lira, not even a ticket back to Frisco."

"Oh," he said.

"Herb Caen would shit his britches if he heard me call it Frisco. I deal with too goddam many sailors. It's not what I like, but it buys the groceries."

"Good."

"Albert," the fat man said. "Albert's the name." He held his hand out across the little table. The waiter put a bottle of beer on each side of it.

"Tommy." Only this morning in the Piazza Venezia he had heard an American woman telling another American woman, "Bob says Eyetalian beer is not bad, and if Bob says it's not bad, you can bet it's not bad." Beyond her loomed the grandiose monument to Victor Emmanuel; it had the strut of Mussolini, who used to gesture like a puppet from the balcony over the woman's head, with little wooden heads crowding the square, arms going up all pulled by the same string. "Bob says that Victor thing is the best thing in Rome," the woman said. "That and the terminal Mussolini built." Near Amalfi he had teetered on the edge of a mountain high above the blue sea, had ridden an elevator down with a sullen man, had boarded a small square boat at the mouth of a cave, had seen sunlight come blue as glass up through the water, had heard stalagmites named: "And that ees Mussolini." A tiny figure, chest and rump out, chin cocked, arm and fist raised, black against the hidden artificial light. Formed and ridiculed by nature long centuries before his birth. Immortal. Il Duce. Dunce.

Dunderhead. "Bob says he was a great man; he got the trains running on time."

"Tommy," Albert was saying. "Thomas. Tomaso. What can I do for you?"

A leaf drifted down from a sycamore tree and landed beside his beer. The leaf was brown and dry. It wasn't autumn yet; it was hardly summer. And the beer was not Italian beer: Imported from Holland, the label said in English. He licked his lips. "The Sistine Chapel. . . ."

"San Tomaso," Albert said. "It was San Tomaso I did on that Eyetalian's back. 'Listen,' I told him, 'art's art, and I'll put the best saint down your backbone anybody ever looked over his shoulder at in a mirror, but don't kid yourself with all this religion. Tomaso's in the cold, cold ground.'" Albert did not pour his beer into the dripping glass the waiter had placed in front of him. He gave the bottle a glance which seemed to say, All right, I see you, and poured it down his throat. He wiped his mouth with the back of his hand. "He didn't get it, of course. Didn't know the song. Me, I grew up in the South. Started out in Norfolk with a specialty in four-leaf clovers on the left hind cheek. Jesus, what I didn't know in those days."

"The Sistine Chapel," he said again.

"We having another beer?" Albert motioned to the waiter. "Due birre. Make it quattro." He closed one eye and stared with the other. It was bulbous and blue, so far as it could be seen a perfect sphere. "Now, what the hell is this about the Sistine Chapel?"

"I want it. On my head."

Albert rolled his lips into his mouth, first the top one, then the bottom. "On your old bald head."

"Yes. Just as if, you know, I had stuck my head up into the dome and the paint had printed itself on my scalp."

Albert sat still a moment. "In reverse," he said.

He thought about it. "I suppose it would have to be."

"Tomaso, Tomaso! Have you ever seen the Sistine Chapel?"

"It was closed. It's closed every Sunday. But . . . I've heard of it, of course."

Albert leaned as far into the little table as his fat would let him. "Well, I'd better inform you, my friend, that your head would no more fit the ceiling of the Sistine Chapel than one of the marbles you've lost would fit my landlady's claw-footed bathtub."

"To scale," he said. "I mean to scale."

"To scale my ass. I'm trying to tell you that the Sistine Chapel ain't got no dome. It's shaped more like the inside of an Arkansas watermelon cut in half lengthways and spooned clean down to the rind."

The sycamores rustled. Zaccheus, he thought. A small motorcycle ground through the beeping traffic and blasted past, numbing his ears. He put his hand to his head, felt it carefully. It certainly was not long like a watermelon, but, then, it was not dome-shaped either. It was broad and round except for a sort of ridge down the middle. He could feel his heart pounding. "It wouldn't have to come down to my ears, would it?"

Albert's eyes moved speculatively to the bald pate before him. The waiter lifted each bottle, took away the empty ones.

"I've seen it," Albert said finally. "For some goddam Christian reason it's free on the last Saturday of every month. Never got poked and shoved by so many people in my life, all looking up. You got a ball point?"

He felt in his jacket pocket, withdrew the pen, clicked it open, handed it to Albert. The bulbous blue eyes had not left his head.

"Lean over."

The ball point ran an elongated course around the ridge of his skull.

"It's about like that. Not perfect. But, hell, Michelangelo didn't have it so easy either. You want this last beer?"

He could never come right out, but now and then while Albert worked he would try to tell him some of it. Once he said that when they shot Jack Kennedy he had cried for three days, but Albert, hoisted above him face down on the scaffolding, had said, "I never could see what was so great about Kennedy. Now, William Howard Taft—there was a man of substance." Albert was in great spirits. "All that agony and ecstasy stuff—hell, give me only ecstasy." That was why he used a vast woven hammock for his scaffolding.

"It seemed like there was hope, then," he told Albert long enough afterward for him not to know it was about Jack Kennedy. And still later, "I decided that I had to be worth shooting by the time I was forty-six." The gentle northern sky settled upon him through the slanted panes, and Albert's rolling laugh, and the familiar prick-prick of the needle upon his skull.

"You want me to put in the cracks?" Albert said.

He thought a moment. "Will it hurt?"

"Jesus Christ. I wasn't planning to use a chisel."

"Well . . . yes." He had learned to talk by moving his lower jaw only, so that his head remained steady. "Exactly the way it is."

"Worth shooting," Albert said. "Down South we used to say not-wuff-a-shit."

"I've got till fall."

He tried to tell about the thumbs, too, how he was walking aimlessly down a street in Palermo, and there she was, this scrawny old woman in a long dress on some steps with her right hand out for money and her two thumbs cocked up, one above the other. Just sitting there, still, saying nothing, not moving.

"Not even twiddling?" Albert said. "Oh, great Christ, she could have been hitchhiking around the world in forty days."

"And then I went to the Catacombe dei Cappuccini."

"Or digging for buggers in both nostrils at once!"

"And this live monk led me down into some long corridors and left me to look at all the dead monks."

"Or fumbling an easy fly in Candlestick Park!"

"They're dried, you know, and hung on the walls."

"Or doing thumbnail sketches for Eyetalians with double vision!"

"Sometimes the cheeks have drawn up and hardened into laughter, or more like minstrels trying to coax you to laugh, the bodies bent and bowing, softshoeing dead still, and hung with old black coats and striped pants."

"Why, she could have been thumbtacking, thumb-sucking, thumbing her nose. . . ."

"You're not listening."

"Oh, yes I am, Mr. Bones." The needle stopped. It was as if time itself were suspended. Albert cleared his throat. "Why did the Cappuccini get to the other side? They rode the cross. Chuckle-chuckle-chuckle."

It was useless. Useless. But he had to finish. "Not all of them are monks. One is a little girl more than fifty years old now, and she looks just the way she did the day she died."

Albert's great fist appeared above him, tugged a rope, pulled his scaffolding into view, the face bulging around its bands of elastic, the eyepiece matching fiercely with a globular blue eye. "Why don't you do what every other forty-five-year-old failure I know does? Go out and make an ass of yourself over some twenty-two-year-old with one thumb on each hand and one boob on each side?"

He had sat stock-still, as though the needle were still going prick-prick on his scalp. "Aurora her name was," he said to the northern light, "as sure as my name is Tommy."

"Well, it's the big day," Albert said. "We'll just see if you got your money's worth. Sit down." He began to unwind gauze just as he did every morning.

One day at the English Tea Room beside the Spanish Steps a woman at the next table had pointed to the swathed head. "A crash upon the motorways," she said. "It's God's judgment upon us." Her remaining teeth were long and kept wanting to slide out over her lower lip. All of her was settled into a shapeless blue dress. "The same as my husband, proud man that he was. Crushed his skull like a melon, they said, when he took his leap through the windscreen and struck the pavement."

"Killed him?" he inquired, unable to say nothing.

"Dead. It was a porker he'd run across, a gross fat porker with a score or so of gross fat dugs like he'd always had a weakness for, all in a double line down her belly. Bruised her something dreadful, and the motor totally demolished."

"Your husband's name was Bob," he told her as if it were only a lucky guess.

She shrieked with laughter. "Not as he ever admitted. Harold, like the Prime Minister. I told my sister at the service, I said, 'Lady,' I said, 'now the two with like names has got heads of equal soundness,' I said, 'only the one's in hell and the other in 10 Downing.' Of course, he'd cleared 10 Downing before a year had gone. It's the darker races causes the trouble, and the poor. If they didn't kill each other off, they'd die of filth and disease, them that hadn't starved. So what's the difference, hey? What's the difference?"

Albert twirled the end of the gauze in the air like a banner and touched the scalp with gentle fingers. He was humming an old-time revival hymn. "I'd sing the goddam words if I could remember them," he said. "This is a serious moment." Overhead he had rigged a magnifying shaving mirror. Onto the base of a music stand he had screwed a round side mirror from an automobile. He placed it grandly into position. "All right, Tomaso," he cried. "Focus!"

His hand was surprisingly calm. You have confidence, he told himself. A little to the left, a little down. . . .

"Head up!" Albert bellowed. "Jesus, you'll see it on the bias!"

Steady, he told himself. Head upright, both hands upon the mirror as though driving, a little more to the left and then farther down . . . and there it was, clear for an instant only before tears blurred the outstretched finger of God only a pore or two from the outstretched finger of Adam.

"I could have done the Last Judgment down your forehead," Albert said, "if you wouldn't keep it wrinkled up all the time."

He held still until he could begin to see again. "It's a beautiful job." He tried to think of another word, but he could not. "Beautiful."

"Well, after all, " Albert said, "I *am* the Tattoo King of the Western World."

"You speak English?" he said. He had missed the banks, had come to the Central Station to cash a traveler's check.

The man in the bright yellow jacket looked up at him. Water ran from the dark hair over the staring face. He had just splashed himself at the lavatory and said God-damn-mother-fucking-son-of-a-bitch. Now he said, "Hell yes. American?"

He nodded. "I'm looking for a lawyer. One that speaks English."

"Son of a bitch," the man said, looking for something to dry his face on. "I haven't slept for two days and the stupid bastards don't even have towels in the john." He jerked a handkerchief from his pocket and swabbed his face violently. "Backward? Keerist! I'm late for a wedding in Messina. Cousin of mine. Flew to Rome and the line at customs was so long I missed my fucking plane, so I grabbed the first one down here, and now there's some kind of son-of-a-bitching strike and I can't get out of the goddam station." He held out his hand. "Charlie," he said. "I own a restaurant in Boston. I told them, I said, 'The problem with you guys is you'll always be screwed up.' Lazy. Fuzzy in the head, you know? Can't focus on getting the job done. 'Jesus,' I told them, 'I drive a seven-thousand-dollar car, and you guys fart around in little Fiats with fourteen kids packed in like sardines.' You know what I mean?"

A Highly Ramified Tree

"A lawyer," he said, "here in Palermo, who speaks English."

"Sure," he said. "I got a cousin works for one. We'll go eat first and get a taxi over there. You like fish?"

At the osteria, Charlie said, "Calamari," and later, "Scampi," and still later, "Spada," and ate all that and a salad of tomatoes and lettuce and olives and fine pink anchovies, and a couple of loaves of bread, and drank a litre and a half of wine. "You know what they'll get for this? Maybe a buck and a half a serving, maybe ten bucks in all for the both of us. Me, I'd get twenty-five, thirty, forty bucks plus the wine. They don't know nothing, for the love of God." He motioned impatiently to the waiter, "You! Il conto! Can't even get them to take your money. Am I glad I left this dump. Il conto!" He looked at the written figures and glared at the waiter. "Four thousand!" he said. "Jesus, that's nearly seven dollars!" He launched into a tirade in Italian; the waiter shouted back; hands flew. After a while Charlie turned and winked. "Give him three thousand," he said. "They got no sense of values."

"The lawyer," he said.

"Oh, yeah. Got something to write on? I'll give you his name and address."

He had not intended to deal with a lawyer. It had all seemed simple, inevitable, when he caught the plane back to Palermo. He had rung the bell at the entrance to the catacombs. In a moment the door opened and a monk stood in it, bearded and silent. Perhaps it was the same one he had seen before; he did not know. He handed the monk a large magnifying glass, removed his hat, bowed his head. He saw the hand dangling from the full brown sleeve go rigid, heard the voice rise in wonder, a single word, musical and sustained: "Sistina!" He had been led inside, settled upon a chair, surrounded with a curtain of brown, pored over, exclaimed over, felt, admired. When he left, he did not know what had been done. A lawyer, he had said to himself in despair. I'll have to get a lawyer.

"American, yes?" the lawyer said. "Ciro sent you? Charlie?" He held out his hand. "I will serve you as best I may." He pressed a button on his desk. A man stuck his nose in the door. "Caffè," he said.

"I want you to deal with the Cappuccini," he said. "I want to be . . . accepted."

The lawyer smiled. "You wish to serve God?"

"No. No. In the catacombs."

"Ah. That will be difficult."

"Just tell them the man with the Sistine Chapel on his head."

The lawyer laughed. "And—how you say it?—the world upon his shoulders?"

He took off his hat and tilted slightly. The lawyer got to his feet behind the desk. "Maria!" he said, crossing himself. "Will it—how you say?—will it wash?"

As before, when the silent man had brought coffee, the lawyer turned his up and downed it with a single swallow. "I admit some difficulty," he said, "but I have told you the best I can the contract. Is not okay?"

He was stricken. The terms seemed to specify that his death must be by lightning, wind, flood, fire, disease, old age, starvation, failure of the vital organs, or some other act of God; or as the result of unavoidable acts of man such as war, the malpractice of doctors, assassination, or error in the construction or operation of aircraft, motorcars, ships, tramways, or other devices mechanical or electrical, provided that the portion of the head bearing the semblance of the ceiling of the Sistine Chapel were intact and in good color. "But," he said, "all of this seems designed to rule out suicide."

"Dio mio," the lawyer said, crossing himself. "Do you know nothing of the laws of God?" He spread his hands. "There are many ways to die. Only one is a mortal sin."

"But . . ." he said, and sat helpless.

The lawyer watched him a moment, stood, opened the window.

Outside there were trees half bare of their leaves, cloth banners strung across the street, left over from the elections. "A magistrate was shot to death near the catacombe, in the spring. Mafia perhaps? His driver too." He pointed; the banner said No Al Caos. Beyond it was visible another with hammer and sickle. "The democrazie have been— how you say?— slipping to the left." He made a motion downward and sideways with his hands. "That is why the fascisti came so strong in the election. We are a stupid people. We need someone to tell us what to do, or nothing is done." He sat back down, was quiet a moment, winked. "To suicide oneself was in the thought, non è vero? A technicality." He tossed it carelessly over his shoulder, then he pointed to his head—his temple? his eye?—and smiled. "For every man, there is a man willing to kill—if reason is given."

He realized that he still held the small cup of coffee. He tasted it, and it seemed to bring his whole head alive. "The Mafia," he said.

The lawyer shook his head violently. "No-no-no-no-no-no. There is no Mafia, and if there is, why do they wish to kill you?"

"Then . . . who?"

The lawyer smiled again. "I have a cousin in the carabinieri who is to be very helpful by reason of his everyday association with . . ." He held his arms out, crossed as though bound at the wrists.

"Don't tell me who," he had said, "as long as he will do it, and do it at the right time."

"No one knows anything," the lawyer had replied, "but he has killed before and wishes to perform well. He will of course be recaptured afterward and returned to the place from which he has been escaped."

Now he sat in the only chair in the sparse room, looking at

his executioner seated upon the narrow bed, astonished that
he should have happened upon so notorious a personage. "So
you are Bertram R. . . ."

"Shhh," the other man said. "We better not use real names.
Call me something else."

"Harvey?" he said.

The man nodded. He was small and very white. His glasses
glinted when he turned beneath the single weak light bulb.
He had hijacked a plane bound from Barcelona to Rome and
shot two Arabs whom, the papers had said, he mistook for
Jews. Since one bullet struck the radio equipment, he managed to get off the plane long enough to mutilate a man who
offered to sell him a gold watch on the street. He had been
startled to find himself in Sicily; he had meant Messina, New
York, where one of his uncles was buried. The first thing he
had done upon coming into the room was ask for water,
which now he sipped and swished about in his mouth. His jaw
was set slightly forward like that of a dog. "I am very religious," he said. "I don't mean in the usual way. That's a lot of
bullshit. I believe in God."

"That's all right."

"And Jesus. I believe in Jesus too. I can paint Jesus Saves in
three languages."

"Three," he murmured.

"Counting English. You probably wonder why I believe in
God but say bullshit."

He shrugged. His hour was near. "The hippies do it."

Harvey stared at him through the thin lenses of his glasses.
His eyes were very blue. "The God damned hippies. It's all
right to say God damn. Only God *can* damn; did you ever
think of that?" He rubbed a hand over his crewcut blond
head. "God reserved long hair for women and beards for
prophets and apostles. I'm a latter-day disciple." He leaned
forward, "I've got to explain it to you. It's a sin to kill one of
your own kind without explaining it to him. I wouldn't feel
right. God would take away my joy."

He looked at his watch. "Of course."

"I've studied," Harvey said. "I only went through the seventh grade, but I paid attention. Before I found God I became a follower of the Japanese mystic Hayakawa, who taught about how the word is not the thing, and I knew why my mouth wanted to say shit and my asshole wouldn't let go. You understand? God lets us learn from the heathen. In the beginning was the Word." He stood up, put his hands into his overcoat pockets, sat down. "It's all right to say bullshit. It's all right to say shit and fuck. God *wants* us to, because those are functions of the natural body, and we have to know about them to keep from doing them." He rubbed his nose with his hand. "I'm a sinner, just like Peter."

The light was dim. Through the threadbare gauze curtains, if the wooden shutters were open, whatever light there was would throw faint patterns on the vaulted ceiling. He was calm. Yesterday he had become forty-six years old, today he would be shot precisely eight years after Jack Kennedy, tomorrow he would be delivered to the Cappuccini for drying and eventual display. He looked at his watch again. "You do have the gun?" he said. Seven-thirty here would be 12:30 Dallas time.

Harvey stood up and checked his overcoat pockets. "Yeah. The knife too." He sat down. "Just like Peter," he said, leaning forward. "You know what your peter is, don't you? And all that about the cock crew—you know what he really did, don't you?"

The only picture on the wall was a garish madonna, hung at a careless angle. In Capri a boy pointed out, far down in the Marina Piccola, the yacht of Jackie and Aristotle Onassis. The boy assisted the waiter at the small hotel; he worked there for six months and on the mainland for six months, twelve, sixteen hours a day to learn the trade, to make something of himself. He wanted to practice his English. "I saw them in the piazza last night," he said. "I do not like Onassis."

"Why not?"

The boy shrugged. "Because he is old and rich."

Madonna, he thought. Mary, wife and mother of us all. Jackie, Coretta, Ethel. At least he himself would never be old. Jesus, Jack, Martin, Bobby. "Just call me Tommy," he heard himself saying.

"All have sinned," Harvey said. "Jesus died for us, and that takes care of the sins of the body, thank God for that. But our whole nation has sinned. I mean the United States. I read about it in the *Reader's Digest* and it hit me like a brick that it was true."

"It's nearly time," he said. "Do you need to cock the gun or something?"

Harvey took the pistol from his pocket, looked at it, snapped something with his thumb. "Just the safety. But don't you see, the sacrifice can't be just anybody and just any old way. God won't work like that. When they first asked me, I said no. I said I got nothing against the Eyetalians, now that I found out the Vatican is a different country, and wasn't it the Eyetalians fought against the black anti-Christ down in Ethiopia? It was when they said you're a white American that God moved me to do it." He laid the pistol on the bed and drew from his other pocket a bonelike handle. Casually he touched it with his thumb and a long thin blade flicked out. "I thought I'd shoot you first."

"Yes," he said. Then, "First?"

"Before taking the scalp. It's the Indians we've sinned against, the lost tribes of Israel God placed in the New World. God trained me up for it, without my knowledge even, from childhood. They used to always be the cowboys and make me be the Indian, and I was the one got shot and tied up and they would run off and leave."

He pulled his hat down as tightly as he could. "But you can't take the scalp," he said. "My head has to be saved."

Harvey stared at him. "Saved? God doesn't save heads."

"He wants mine saved. Just the way it is."

"But it won't do any good without the scalp. Don't you understand? It's for the Indians."

"No," he said. "No. I didn't agree to that."

Harvey stood blinking at him through the glasses. Suddenly he closed the knife and jammed it into his pocket, snatched the gun up off the bed, started for the door. "Well bullshit!" he cried. "Just . . . bullshit!"

He was exhausted. He had walked all night and through the morning. He had staggered in and out of beeping Palermo traffic, had been nudged by tiny Fiats, been shouted at, gestured at, accosted. He had gone through dark alleyways, down long tree-lined streets, beside a waterfront crowded with boats and crusted with road construction. He had stopped at a little fish market and stared at the swordfish cut neatly in two, one half hung sword up, the other half facing him, a perfect circle of translucent flesh patterned around the symmetrical bone.

I must think, he had said to himself from time to time, but he had not thought. Now, with a warm November sun in his eyes, he saw ahead of him the same steps he had seen long before, the same woman in the same long dress, the same two thumbs standing one above the other, cocked rigidly upon the hand held as though casually to receive money. He stood a moment over her, uncertain what to do. His legs ached, his breath hurt his chest, his head dripped with sweat. Abruptly, he sat down. From his back pocket he took out his handkerchief, ran it over his forehead and cheek, wiped the back of his neck. He took off his hat and sponged the sweat from his head. For a moment he sat still, panting. Then he put his hat in his lap and began with both hands carefully to fold the handkerchief. It was some time before he realized that coins were falling into his hat, that voices were saying, "Bello! Favoloso! Meraviglioso!" He could not bring himself to move.

His eyes stayed upon the play of coins falling, the pile rising in the hat. He was only distantly aware that a man had begun to charge for the use of a magnifying glass.

His legs did not want to unbend. "Wait," he said. "Wait," trying to unlock the stiff muscles, but a thin strong hand was tugging him to his feet. It was, he began to realize, the left hand of the old woman; it had only one thumb.

She said things, but he did not understand them. As they walked he held the hat out toward her and said, "For you," but she seemed to ignore him. The skin of her face was as parched and tight as that of a dried monk. They turned down a narrow street, walked through a tiny courtyard, climbed narrow stairs in the dark.

She set him upon a stool and pulled back a dingy curtain; he saw a washstand, a single butane burner, a comb and brush. She took the hat and turned her back; he heard the rush of coins into something he could not see. Then she stopped, peering and fumbling into the base of the washstand, and came up with a rag and a scrub brush. Now she stood before him, held out her right hand, said something.

"What?" he said, "I don't speak Italian."

She said it again, vehemently, pointing with her left forefinger at the two thumbs. All he got was Dio.

"Oh," he said after a moment. "God. God gave you that?"

She pointed to his head and rattled off something negative—he got the non—about Dio.

"God didn't give me this? No. Nor much else."

She took the rag in her left hand and grasped the brush firmly in her right, fingers tight upon the wooden back against the opposing thumbs. He sat in shock for some moments before he realized that it was a wire brush, that the drops she was wiping at upon his forehead, around his ears, were blood. He sat as still as he could.

15 *The Old Man*

Here are your waters and your watering place.
Drink and be whole again beyond confusion.

—Robert Frost

I feel as though I am coming awake from a nightmare: the months in Europe, the agonizing struggle to break away, the dividing up of a household piece by piece. My home now is the Volkswagen camper, shipped over from Germany. It is parked in the driveway beside the house near Clinton, where I grew up.

I am sitting on the couch in the living room, where I sometimes used to sit close beside my father, helping him work the crossword puzzle. It is not the old wicker davenport; only the upright piano is what and where it used to be. I can hear my parents' voices, my father asking something from out back, my mother replying through the kitchen window.

The back yard is no longer fenced in for chickens; there is no lot for cows, no enclosed garden with old peach trees big enough to climb. Now St. Augustine grass is thick under the huge pecan tree which had yet to sprout when we moved away thirty years ago; the green lawn spreads far back, broken only by other pecan trees, pear trees, apple trees, a few grapevines, a muscadine arbor. Afternoons we sit in the swing and in lawn chairs in the cool green shade. Sometimes my father gets caught up in the sermon he has been forming in his head and has no pulpit for, and I stand until my back aches while he preaches it to me, my head among pecan leaves, my feet on one of the flagstones laid between the back door and the tool shed he has had made from the old garage. Beyond it, where the higher part of the pasture used to be, is a large garden with rows of green beans, butter beans, squash, okra, eggplant, onions, lettuce, tomatoes, peppers, field peas.

"I think that garden save my life," he has told me. When they returned from Kentucky he expected to be kept busy with revivals, but invitations were very sparse. He was seventy. In the fifteen years he was out of circulation, the generation of preachers had changed. Only a few years before, my brothers and sister and I had talked of making signs to wear wherever in the South we went: Yes, Brother Joe Is My Father. Everybody asked, eyes lighting up with remembered pleasure. When he came home full of sermons and songs no one asked to hear, he put all his energy into the soil. One season the tomatoes he was giving away weighed up to four pounds each.

At seventy-five he was asked to teach a couple of courses at the black seminary in Jackson. He studied the history and psychology texts they gave him with the same thoroughness he brought to any written words. Soon it was lectures on how the mind works, out there on the flagstones, as often as sermons. He loved the work, loved the people he was dealing with. He hung on to the job until my mother had to go along to drive, to write things on the board for him, to bring him back to the lesson when he wandered into some story of his childhood; until finally he sat with his students and she taught the class.

Now, on the couch in the living room of my old home, I am hardly aware of the argument going on through the kitchen window. I have my own argument going with my mother, in my head, over what my father may not have been told, what she and I have kept silent about all during this visit: Separation. Impending divorce. Marriage to a girl half my age. Allegiances shift, I tell her. What about Dad, who owed allegiance to an Italian king and became an ardent citizen of the United States, who owed allegiance to the Pope and became a Southern Baptist preacher? Why is it good that he abandoned one country for another, one faith for another, and bad that I abandon one woman for another, and a faith in what I had been told for a belief in what I could perceive, with no less sense of inevitability, of arriving where I have to be?

The voices have grown so much louder and more impatient that I can no longer ignore them. I go back through the house to mediate. "You don't need it, Joe," my mother is calling out the window as I come into the kitchen.

He shouts something I cannot make out, from the darkness of the shed.

"What's he after," I say.

"Another extension cord. He's got one that reaches to the shed doorway, but he wants to be able to run the grill under cover if it rains."

My brother and his family are coming over, and my father will barbecue supper for us. He has an electric charcoal starter. I go out to help.

He has spotted the extension cord, at last, the proper outdoor kind, looped high on the shed wall. I move a ladder to it, take it down, plug it into the one already stretched out from the house. He is so irritated that his feet stomp the ground at every step. He lines up the portable grill with the shed door, takes aim, rolls it carefully in, looks up to see that it is well under the roof, rolls it carefully out. Then he steps back and looks up at me, lips compressed. His hands go into motion.

"You mother," he begins. He takes a deep breath and starts

over. "You mother, she'sa think I got some of this . . . What
you call it when you get old? Senility. She'sa think I got some
senility." He spreads his hands out in acceptance. "All right
I'va got some senility. But I take it into consideration."

It grows steadily worse, although there are times when he is
as lucid as in the old days: he gives a perfectly coherent ex-
planation when I say, "Mafioso," pointing to the cap set
rakishly on his head.

"No," he tells my brother, "that'sa not mean I'm in the
Mafia. It means I try looka tough." He swaggers a little, draws
his mouth down, laughs. "I'ma not mafioso. I wear my cap on
side of my head so it won't press this little sore spot on my
forehead. But," he shrugs, "you do what you do, it looks the
way it looks."

When my new wife is there for the first time, however, at
Christmas, he tells about when Jesus was born and casually
remarks, "Me and this other fellow walk over there and see
him." We cannot tell whether he knows what this girl is doing
here with me.

By his eighty-eighth year, he has begun to wander off from
the house occasionally. When we visit that summer, bringing
our old English sheepdog, my wife sits with him under the
big pecan tree while I help my mother with something in the
house. The dog is lying on the grass in front of them. My
father's face begins to look remote, as if he is drifting away.
My wife looks around for something to keep his attention.

"Do you like dogs?" she asks him. He has petted Micawber
before, scratching his ears and his neck methodically, as if he
is obliged to do a thorough and complete job of it.

He pulls himself into focus. "Huh?"

"Dogs. Do you like them?" She is pointing at Micawber.

He stares. "That thing?" He seems to study Micawber for a
while. Finally he says, "We can't be responsible for the souls of
all the animals." He pauses, still fixed on the dog. "I would
speak to him about Christ, but I'm afraid it would confuse
him."

That afternoon we drive to Vicksburg. On the way I get lost trying to find the post office in Clinton. It has been moved a couple of times since it was right downtown when I was a boy; I drive up beside the latest building I know of and get out with a handful of letters. "Where are you going?" my mother asks.

"To mail these."

"This isn't the post office anymore. It's down where Miss Jessie Harris used to live."

I pull into the parking lot there, go into the large new building, wander around corners among a maze of boxes until I find the counter. When I go outside I am in the wrong parking lot; I have to search out the car.

"What's happened to this place?" I say. It used to be a town of about a thousand people, with elms lining brick streets in which everybody walked, the way they stroll in the piazza at Palazzo.

"It's certainly changed. They say the population is more than seventeen thousand now." We drive west past a low building which seems endless. "I don't know what this is," my mother says. "Some industry or other."

In the battlefield park, my father is apprehensive. He has it in his head that we're taking him somewhere to leave him. My mother is patient with him, keeps reassuring him. He worries that the car will go off the narrow road, which drops abruptly beside his window, is afraid that I won't stop in time as I nose into a parking place in Fort Hill, overlooking the Yazoo basin far below. "Why are we going here?" he asks plaintively as we drive through the floodwall onto the sloping concrete levee.

"To see the canal," I tell him.

"Who wants to see the canal?" he says, and then, "Who wants to see the river?" when I mention we will go to a turnout near the bridge over the Mississippi.

As I twist and turn through little streets, he begins to come out of it. "You don't know where you're going," he tells me. "Why you want to go on this street?" His voice is no longer plaintive; he is picking at me, turning his earlier apprehension into a joke.

I swing around the mound of earth that was once a gun emplacement, park in the semicircle overlooking the river. The water is low; a wide stretch of sand is visible on the Louisiana side. My mother, sitting between us, says, "Look, Joe. Look at the river."

He keeps his eyes straight ahead. "I don't want to look at the river. What you want look at a river for?"

"It's a great view, from here," I say.

"Yes," my mother says. "Look, Joe."

"I not gonna look." He bites his lip, cuts his eyes toward her briefly.

My mother pushes at his face playfully, tries to turn his head toward where the river curves away from us. He resists; his shoulders shake with held-in laughter. "I not gonna look at any river."

I am struck by the view: the river flowing under the bridge and sweeping in a wide curve westward just where, from my vantage point, my father's stubborn face is set toward the source. He is wearing the dark cap he seems never to forget I gave him. When he first tried it on he laughed: This makes me look like an old Italian. My mother laughed too: What do you think you are?

My wife has climbed the grassy mound to get a better look. When I join her I can see that I have had the world all turned around again; the river is actually coming toward us out of the west, curving to flow down under the bridge. The late sun glints off the moving water.

When I get back into the driver's seat, my father turns to me; the senility seems fully taken into consideration, the flow of blood full to the brain. Out of nothing, yesterday, he has said to me with this same clear look, I may be old, but I'm still here. This time he says, "We going home now?"